IN THE BLINK OF AN EYE

IN THE BLINK OF AN EYE

The Reed and Rob Nixon Story

SHERYL BROWN NIXON

Outskirts Press, Inc.
Denver, Colorado

In The Blink of An Eye
The Reed and Rob Nixon Story
All Rights Reserved.
Copyright © 2011 Sheryl Brown Nixon
v4.0

Front Cover photograph of Reed and Rob in wheelchairs courtesy Busath Photography

Outskirts Press, Inc.
http://www.outskirtspress.com

ISBN: 978-1-4327-6925-3

Outskirts Press and the "OP" logo are trademarks belonging to Outskirts Press, Inc.

PRINTED IN THE UNITED STATES OF AMERICA

Acknowledgements

Shortly after I began writing this book my husband, Mark and I were at an extended family reunion in Idaho when one of his cousins, Bobby Johnson came up to me, handed me two twenty-dollar bills, and said, "Here is the money for a copy of your book when it is done." That was over three years ago. I have carried that forty dollars in my purse these past three years as a constant reminder that Bobby had paid me for a book and I needed to keep at it until I had one for him.

His prepaying for my book has been a big motivation to complete it. Thank you, Bobby!

In the beginning, Cheryl Carson really helped me get organized and start the actual book publishing process. Her help was so valuable to me.

When I finally had a working manuscript, my sister, Marnae Wilson helped me incredibly by editing and polishing my thoughts and words on paper. I couldn't have finished this book without her help.

Katie Nixon was wonderful in helping me maintain a focused story line. Her suggestions and comments really pulled the story together with a theme and purpose.

My husband, Mark and all of my children and their

spouses have been instrumental in making sure I got my facts straight, especially Reed and Rob. Thank you all.

I also owe a debt of gratitude to the many other friends and family who read early drafts of the book and made valuable suggestions.

I love you all very much! Thank you again.

When sorrow comes we have no right to ask,
"Why did this happen to me?"
Unless we ask the same question for every
Moment of happiness that comes our way.

Author Unknown

Contents

1984 Robert and Reed – Best Friends

1994 Last family photograph before accident

CHAPTER **1**

"JUST A SECOND Brent, I have another call...." I pushed the flash button on the telephone and said, "Hello."

"Hello, Mrs. Nixon. Umm...we've been in a car accident. It happened on the way home from the church. Two of the kids are being airlifted to the University of Massachusetts Medical Center [UMASS] in Worcester as soon as the emergency crews can get them out of the van."

I blinked.

I knew my children's friends loved to tease me; I hoped beyond all hope that it wasn't true. I tentatively asked him, "Are you kidding?" He wasn't.

I pushed the flash button again to get back to my brother Brent and told him my kids and their friends had just been in a car accident. I explained to him that emergency crews were trying to remove two of them from the van to be flown to the hospital. I hadn't been told which two. Realizing it was a very serious accident, Brent said he'd talk to me later, hung up the phone, and called our extended family members to let them know what had happened.

I learned about the accident at 9:20 p.m. on Tuesday, April 4, 1995. Four of our six children—Reed, Robert, Natalie, and Kent—had left home at 7:00 that evening with four of their friends to go to a church youth activity. Where were they now? What had happened? I immediately telephoned my husband, Mark, who was working late at Bentley University, to let him know the kids had been in a wreck.

Grabbing my keys, I dashed out to the garage to get in the van when I realized it was gone! Of course! The kids had driven it to the church for their activity! I rushed back into the house and called my neighbor to ask if I could borrow her car. She offered to go with me, but I told her I was just going to pick the kids up and bring them home—I never thought they might be hurt badly enough that they wouldn't *be able* to come home.

I flew through the night toward Marlborough where the accident had happened, twenty-five minutes away, glancing in my rearview mirror at a vehicle shadowing my every move, wondering if it belonged to the parents of one of the other children in the accident. I grieved for those parents, knowing that they would be as terrified as I was, and I worried about how seriously *my* children may have been injured. I noticed an ambulance screaming toward me with blazing lights. I wondered as it passed whether it held any of my children.

Arriving at the scene of the accident with the car behind me screeching to a halt too, I was blinded by red, yellow, and blue flashing lights from police cars and other emergency vehicles. I stared, unable to blink. I wanted to turn away from the frightful scene, but I had to look for my kids!

A chill ran through my bones as I frantically searched for my children. When I climbed into the ambulance nearest me, my heart skipped a beat. I saw my Natalie, lying on a stretcher, a cervical collar around her neck, sobbing. With no time to answer my questions, the paramedic asked me to leave. I felt a tear trickle down my cheek as my eyes followed her ambulance, screaming away into the night. Gathering every ounce of my strength and courage, I set off—heart racing—to find my other children.

I rounded the corner and found our mangled cherry-red

minivan. Bright yellow security tape surrounded the accident area repeating the warning, "Police Line Do Not Cross," which prevented me from getting closer to Reed, whom I saw at a distance being carried on a stretcher by paramedics to a waiting ambulance. From what I could see, he looked perfectly normal with no signs of trauma. He wasn't bloody or crying, just lying still, as if asleep on the stretcher. The ambulance took him to a nearby parking lot where a medical helicopter whisked him away to UMASS.

I was shaking with adrenaline and blinking back the tears as I searched for Robert and Kent. Some of my questions were answered when the police told me that Robert had already been airlifted to UMASS. They told me that it had taken thirty minutes to get him out of the van and sixty minutes to get Reed out. Kent had been taken by ambulance to Framingham Union Hospital a short time earlier, since there had already been too many victims taken to Marlborough Hospital. Reed and Robert's injuries were serious enough that they had to be flown to UMASS, which was much further away.

There I stood out in the cold black night, completely stunned, with four of my children in three different hospitals in three different cities.

Because I was dazed and confused, not able to think of where to go or what to do, my friends at the scene told me to go to UMASS since both Reed and Robert had to be taken there by helicopter. One friend returned my neighbor's car while another drove me to UMASS, about forty-five minutes away. Shortly after leaving for the hospital my friend realized that she didn't have enough gas to get there, so we were forced to pull into a nearby gas station. I was frantic to get to my sons, and it seemed like the pump was delivering one drop of gas at a time. My sons urgently needed me. Like Captain Kirk,

I wanted to demand, "Beam me to the hospital, Scotty," but there I had to sit, a prisoner at the gas station.

That next hour's drive was a total blur, as if I were watching a movie in fast forward. When I finally arrived at UMASS I was surprised and grateful to be met at the Emergency Room (ER) entrance by one of my local church leaders, who took me to a private family waiting room that had been set aside for us. The smells of antiseptic and illness hit me as I entered—my nightmare was just beginning. Where was Mark?

CHAPTER 2

IMMEDIATELY AFTER MY call, Mark had rushed to the scene of the accident, but by the time he arrived there were only a few paramedics there. They told him Reed and Robert were conscious and talking when they last saw them. Mark assumed, as I had initially assumed, that Reed and Robert had only minor injuries, so he decided to go to Marlborough Hospital to check on Natalie, the four friends, and their parents.

Mark sighed with relief when he found (except for one sprained wrist) all of the friends were uninjured. They had been treated and released. Our thirteen-year-old Natalie, however, was in tremendous pain. The doctor put a cervical collar around her neck, gave her some Tylenol to help ease the pain, and sent her home.

Mark left Marlboro Hospital and hurried to Framingham Union Hospital to see how our twelve-year-old son Kent was doing. Kent looked horrible—he had a huge bulge on his forehead, scrapes on his cheeks, and shards of glass stuck into the skin on both sides of his waist. He was afraid, hurting all over, and really relieved to see his dad walk in.

Just after Mark got there, without any anesthetic an ER doctor dug into Kent's skin to remove the chunks of glass. Mark was not impressed with the doctor and the insensitive way Kent was treated. Then another doctor arrived, deadened the area, removed the remaining glass, and stitched Kent up.

A friend from church, whose car had been right behind our van before the accident, spent the night with Kent in the hospital while Mark hurried to UMASS to check on Reed and Robert.

Meanwhile I was waiting to hear how Reed and Robert were doing. Why wasn't I allowed to be with them? I kept asking the nurse what their status was and she continually gave me the same annoying answer: "They're having x-rays, CAT scans, and testing done, so we won't know anything until all of that is completed."

My life was speeding out of control, and the longer I waited the more panicked I got. I was so frustrated! What would I be dealing with?

Only a week before the accident I had said to my close friend Charlene, "If one more stressful thing happens, you can just lock me up in a mental hospital!" When she got word of the accident, she thought I would fall apart and end up in the hospital, too! I was in shock, but surprisingly, I didn't crumble or fall apart. I think I was too numb and too busy being panicked to allow myself the luxury of an emotional breakdown.

At the time of my children's accident I had been diagnosed with chronic depression (a chemical imbalance in the brain) and was seeing a therapist. My depression began after the birth of my sixth child, Kent. Six children in eight years were more than my body could handle. I was so exhausted that I was in bed for much of the day, sleeping for hours at a time.

When I first went to the doctor to find out why I was so exhausted, he asked me if I was depressed. I told him I wasn't; I had a good marriage, great kids, and a new house. What I didn't realize at the time was that just because I was happy didn't necessarily mean I wasn't depressed. Depression can be brought on by good stress as well as bad, and I had plenty of good stress. When I was first put on medication, I took it for a week. I was feeling better, so I threw the rest of the bottle away. The next time I was prescribed medication, I kept the written prescription in my purse for several weeks and finally threw it away. After several months of this, I decided to get a third prescription and *take it*. In the back of my mind, however, I thought I would be well when I got off the medicine. When I began to feel better, I decreased the dose of the medication. As soon as I began feeling worse, I'd raise the dose. I had unknowingly put myself and my family on a terrible roller coaster ride. Finally one day Mark said, "When you feel good maybe you should just continue with the same dose and not change anything."

Sure enough, it worked and I began feeling well for longer periods of time.

However, in 1988, while playing softball, I was struck in the face with a hard-hit ball. I ended up with a spinal fluid leak (diabetes incipitus), two broken teeth, a bruised pituitary gland, and several spider fractures around my mouth and nose. The trauma caused me to get fibromyalgia (a chronic aching of the muscles and tissues). Fibromyalgia causes pain and fatigue, and has many of the same characteristics as depression.

When my sons' accident happened, I was already being treated for these two conditions, so maybe the medication I was taking for the depression and fibromyalgia kept my emotions on an even keel while I waited for Mark to get to the hospital.

I really needed Mark's companionship and strength, but my faith and prayers would have to suffice for the moment. It had been hours and Mark still hadn't arrived. I felt as if I'd been waiting days. I couldn't imagine what was taking him so long. Neither of us had a cell phone, so I couldn't call him, and I had no way of knowing he had gone to the other two hospitals first.

Finally, after more than three hours, I was allowed to visit our son Robert. Mentally preparing myself for what I might find, I held my breath and tip-toed into his room. There he lay, looking so young—barely sixteen. His body looked perfect: not a scratch, no sign of external damage whatsoever. He simply looked as if he were gently sleeping.

I approached him and saw a horrible hose-type thing sticking out of his mouth! It looked like some weird contraption that would stop him from breathing, not help. My first thought was to rip that awful thing out of his mouth and just take him home as I had planned, but then I saw lots of other tubes and hoses poking in and out of his body. My eyes welled up with tears and I silently cried, "No! This can't possibly be happening! This is just a hideous nightmare!"

I felt as though I'd suddenly been thrust into a deep black hole, impossible to escape from, but my motherly instinct to protect Robert was more powerful than my fear, so I tried to pull myself together. I had no idea how badly he was hurt. Robert didn't even know I was there. Visibly shaken, I stumbled out the door back to the waiting room. Then I let out my breath, realizing that this was *not* a nightmare I could wake up from.

Mark arrived—a wonderful sight—and crying, I ran into his arms. The mood in the room was incredibly different from what he expected. He was stunned and confused when I told him what had happened, although we still had yet to understand how critical our sons' conditions actually were.

Eventually a doctor sat us down and gave us a blow by blow account of the injuries our sons' bodies had sustained. The doctor began very carefully as he explained that Reed and

Robert each had collapsed lungs, bruised hearts, and broken necks, resulting in spinal cord injuries. We were both completely shocked! We hadn't even completely registered all of that information when he continued, "They're both paralyzed from the neck down."

What did the doctor just say? Did we hear him correctly? What exactly does it mean to have collapsed lungs and bruised hearts? Paralyzed? He *must* be mistaken! Surely there was *some* way to fix their injuries. This was so unfair! But even as the thought entered my mind, I could hear myself saying to my children years before: "Life isn't fair. Life happens and we have to deal with the challenges when they come." This was my grim reality. I would have to practice what I preached.

Then the doctor continued, "...and neither of them can breathe on their own; they are both on life support."

I wanted to shout, "Stop! Enough!" My brain was crammed with more medical terms than it could take in, and I couldn't concentrate one second more. Mark and I fought back tears, trying to remember what was said and remain as level-headed as possible, but we found ourselves in unknown territory that we could never return from. Faced with such unbelievable circumstances, feeling overwhelmed and incapable of making rational decisions, we began our uncharted journey.

We were finally allowed to look in on our seventeen-year-old son, Reed. He also looked perfect: no cuts, scrapes, or bruises. Then we saw that awful-looking hose sticking out of his mouth, too. In the quiet of the room we watched Reed's chest rise and fall with the hiss of the ventilator in the background breathing for him. Tubes and wires were everywhere, hooking his body up to different monitors: a chest tube drained fluid from his lungs, a pulse/oxygen monitor measured the oxygen level in his blood, IV tubes provided fluids and medications, a Foley catheter collected urine, and another monitor beeped with every beat of his heart.

Medical personnel were continually in and out of the room, and I had no idea what they were doing. Even if they had tried to explain it to me, I wouldn't have understood. I felt as if I were watching a devastating scene from TV's ER, only this time it was real. Seeing my sons with all those tubes, clinging to life there in the ICU, I was afraid *my* life, as well as theirs, was over.

Tears stung my eyes, and I turned away to gain my composure. Numb and dazed, I wondered how my handsome sons could look so normal on the outside and have irreversible damage on the inside. I tried to understand what it all meant, but I just couldn't. And Mark? He was completely shattered! Throughout all the hours of driving from one hospital to the next, he'd thought that his sons would be all right. But they were *not* going to be all right. Everything we had ever known and loved and taken for granted had changed in the blink of an eye.

IT'S HARD TO remember what our day-to-day routine was like before the accident, but sometimes I dream of how it used to be. I'm sitting on the high school bleachers soaking in the sunshine of a magnificent New England autumn afternoon in 1994, shouting at the top of my voice, "Run, Reed! Go, Robert! Leave it all on the field!" Running like the wind, they win their race and help their cross-country team earn the league championship. Panting, with red faces, they beam their satisfaction at having achieved their personal best times, as well as going undefeated throughout the entire season.

Reed 1994 track meet

Then I'm watching a springtime track meet, cheering for Robert until my voice is gone, as he sets the freshman record for the 1600-meter race at five minutes one second. I get emotional as I notice Reed congratulating his brother with a warm smile and gigantic hug.

Robert 1994 track meet

My sons were teammates; I loved watching them interact. Now I would give *anything* to shout my support for them. Just one more time.

Our six children were born between 1975 and 1983. Before we were married, Mark and I decided that six kids sounded like a good number. We both came from large families—Mark's parents had six kids, and mine had seven. We often reminisced about the old days when large families were the norm.

Raelene, our oldest, was born in 1975. Since Mark was the oldest of six boys, and ultrasounds were uncommon, I just assumed we were having a boy and took only boy clothes to the hospital. We were really surprised and happy to find out we had a little girl! I sang to her as I rocked her to sleep.

Beautiful baby, beautiful child.
Beautiful baby, tender and mild.
You are the love, the love of my life.
You are the love of a husband and wife.

Beautiful baby, beautiful child....
I love you so, and I want you to know
You will always be my beautiful baby....

From, Beautiful Baby, Sheryl Nixon, 1997

Renae was born thirteen months later in 1976. These two little girls became such close playmates that Mark and I decided to have all our children in twos. A couple of years later, in 1978, Reed was born, and then Robert followed in 1979. They were just three days short of a year apart. Four children in four years was more demanding than I'd imagined, so we decided to wait a few years before adding more to our family. Natalie was born in 1982, with her best friend and brother, Kent, arriving only thirteen months later. I was completely consumed by the needs of my children.

I woke up this mornin' to the garbage truck roarin'
Down the street. I missed him again.
By this time next week that trash will reek,
And I'll need oxygen.
I've got the floor to mop from that can of pop

Spilled the night before.
My baby, who is barely two,
Is smearin' lipstick on the door.
I've got the midweek housewife blues....

From, Midweek Housewife Blues, Sheryl Nixon, 1985

Just about every memory our children had involved one sibling or another. All they ever knew was each other. Loyalty was a main focus for our family, and we supported each other in everything possible, from attending music and dance recitals or church functions such as choir practices and performances to cheering at various sporting events—soccer, baseball, basketball, football, or tennis. We worked hard and played even harder.

There was hardly a time that our kids didn't have at least one sibling in the same school with them, and they looked out for each other. Six-year-old Natalie was in first grade when she saw her nine-year-old brother Robert in the hall being teased by a classmate. She charged right up, screaming, "You leave my brother alone!" The bully was surprised by this little girl shouting at him, and turned to attack her. Seeing him turn, Robert came to Natalie's rescue. Two against one was more than the boy had bargained for, so he left. Now Natalie would give anything to fight even one of Robert's daily battles.

Our vacations were fun, busy, and chaotic. In 1989, we went to California to see the Rose Parade. A year later we scrimped and saved, and gave up our gift-giving in exchange for a Christmas Eve and Christmas Day at Disney World in Florida. What a blast! Two years after that, we took a US history trip to Washington DC. We had never been to the East Coast before, and on that trip we got a glimpse of what that part of the country was like. That glimpse helped us adjust a couple of years later when we moved to Massachusetts, where the accident happened. We wish now that we had taken the kids on many more vacations, because after the accident travel became very difficult.

As a family, we ate meals, went to church, and had family prayers together. Those simple family activities gave us a strong bond of faith that helped us survive the trauma of the accident. I remember one particular morning years earlier when I was sick. Mark had already left for work, so the kids, who were still little, got their own breakfast. Then they came to the side of my bed for family prayers before leaving for school. They prayed for me to feel better, for them to do well at school, and for Daddy to be fine at work. After the accident our family prayers were much more intense, but the foundation of faith we established those many years ago helped keep our family strong.

As I thought about the possibility that Reed might never walk again, I reflected on a time when he was only five, and asked his dad to take his shoes to his room for him. When Mark said "no," Reed pointed out, "But Dad, I always take *your* shoes up to *your* room for *you!*" Without a word more, Mark returned the favor and took Reed's shoes to his room. Now Mark and I would not only be carrying Reed's shoes, we'd be dressing, bathing, feeding, and carrying him for the rest of his life.

The other day I watched you and your little boy playing games.
Neither of you noticed I was there.
You both were captivated, and I knew I'd never seen
A father-son relationship to compare.

I love to see him sit like you and comb his hair like yours.
Sometimes he tries to read the paper, too.
He brings you down your slippers. Then he says, "Will
you get mine?"
I can tell he's crazy over you.
You're his hero....

Sheryl Nixon, 1986

As children, Reed and Robert were almost always together, whether it was in scouting, sports, or church activities. But
their favorite times were the ones they spent annoying their
sisters. Early on, they perfected the art of teasing. They'd burst
out laughing every time they succeeded in ruffling the girls'
feathers. We were constantly bombarded with laughter mixed
with screaming.

One day when Robert was five and Reed six, our family discovered mice in the basement. The girls found out and
were absolutely terrified! Every morning someone had to
check the mouse traps we had set, so Reed and Robert would
run down the stairs hoping to find a dead mouse. Then they'd
take the mouse out of the trap and swing it by the tail as they
chased their sisters around the house. Their stunts were so
traumatizing that our girls still panic over anything having to
do with mice.

⌡⌡⌡

After we moved to Texas in 1989, Reed and Robert became very involved in scouting, especially since their uncle
Clair was their scoutmaster. During the summers they sold
discount coupons from local businesses to earn enough money to pay their scout camp fees. By the time we left Texas in
1993, Reed and Robert had each achieved the rank of Life

Scout. When we arrived at our new home in Massachusetts, they unloaded the truck and took off the very next day for a week-long, fifty-mile hike across the Appalachian Trail with their new scout troop.

In Massachusetts, Reed and Robert started the school year at Algonquin Regional High School. Reed had a passion for running that had begun in Texas, so as a sophomore he joined the Algonquin cross-country team. He got faster and faster until by the end of the season he received the "Most Improved Runner" award. Reed told Robert what a great time he was having and convinced Robert to run as well. Robert joined the spring track team and his competitive nature kicked in as he ran with Reed. By the time the track season ended in 1994, Robert had won the "Most Improved Runner" award, too.

We made our start a year apart.
Just me an' you was all that we knew.
No matter where, we were a pair.
Brothers together from the heart.

Though we were small, an' not so tall,
We spent our time playin' basketball.
We loved to race, we set the pace,
Stayin' together through it all.

'Cause we've got brotherly love....

From, Brotherly Love, Sheryl Nixon, 1997

By mid-March 1995, both boys were long-distance runners, training and preparing for the upcoming track season. Just three short weeks later, in the blink of an eye, their joy in running was over forever.

CHAPTER  4

THE NIGHT OF the accident, our minivan came to a rest upside down in a clump of trees, facing the opposite direction the boys were traveling. Reed and Robert dangled in their seat belts and shoulder harnesses. Reed knew he was seriously hurt because his legs "were in an awkward, unnatural position" and he couldn't feel them. However, he was the driver of the van and was more concerned for the other passengers than he was for himself.

Where was Robert, his best friend, teammate, and brother? Was he alive? And Natalie, whom he had loved and teased for years, was she okay? What about Kent, how was he? And his friends riding with him? Fearing the worst, he was overwhelmed.

At the time we didn't know what had caused the accident, but several years later we learned that the rear brakes in the van didn't work that night, and actually had never worked. There wasn't any evidence that brake fluid had *ever* been in the brake lines. Since eighty percent of the braking was done with the front brakes and only twenty percent with the rear, we hadn't noticed a problem before the accident. But with the van full of people traveling too fast around a curve, when Reed put the brakes on and didn't have the stabilization normally provided by the rear brakes, the back end of the van jumped and he lost control. Then he sideswiped a telephone pole, hit a curb (sending the van airborne), crashed into some trees, and landed upside down.

Reed and Robert had been riding in the two front seats of the minivan. During the crash, the momentum of the van pushed their bodies forward. Hitting a tree at the same time, the ceiling and windshield collapsed. Reed and Robert's heads hit the collapsed roof, which instantly stopped the forward motion of their heads and snapped their necks. The paramedics had a hard time stabilizing both boys, so they were flown to UMASS where they could get expert care.

Once the ER doctor had given his initial diagnoses, medical personnel moved Reed and Robert into two separate rooms in the Pediatric Intensive Care Unit (PICU), hoping to avoid any potential mix ups with medications and specific care. It looked as if Mark and I would be spending several days there in the PICU, so during the transition we dashed home to grab some clothes. At the last minute, I also grabbed two tape players and two cassette tapes of me singing some of my original songs.

I was already a professional vocalist before our kids were born, but later I discovered I could write my own songs, as well.

Music and I had a type of spiritual connection. Writing music calmed my heart and soul, especially during challenging times. Several years earlier, I sang and recorded a dozen songs I had written.

Both Reed and Robert had early memories of my singing to them, so I decided to put a tape player in each of their rooms, since I couldn't be with them both at the same time. Even so, I felt bad that I couldn't always be there for each of them. But I knew that playing my music was the best way I could connect with them when I wasn't physically able to be by their side. I hoped that my songs would calm their hearts like the songs had mine when I'd written them.

Reed and Robert were in the PICU for three weeks. Early on I was with Robert one afternoon when a nurse came in and explained that Robert's lungs were filling up with fluid and he needed to be turned on his side so his lungs could drain. Would I please leave while that was being done? I was in with Reed only a few minutes when Robert's nurse came in and said, "We just experienced an event with Robert."

An event? What was that? In a matter-of-fact manner she calmly explained that as they were turning Robert, he went into cardiac arrest! Cardio Pulmonary Resuscitation (CPR) was administered and he was stabilized. I blinked.

What? How could his heart have stopped? That happens only to old people! And I wouldn't call that an event! An event is something I'd see at a circus! This was a crisis! The thought of those defibrillator paddles jolting my little boy's chest with electrical shocks was frightening! He was so young and afraid; I felt awful that I hadn't been in his room to comfort him. However, would I have panicked if I had seen and heard the flat line drone of the heart monitor? Maybe it was best that I hadn't been there. Over and over, I worried about each of my injured children. After the "event" with Robert, every moment I feared for his life. And whenever I wasn't with Reed, I was terrified that he might have an "event" too. It was horrible having to choose between one son and another. And how were Natalie and Kent doing? Who was taking care of them?

My heart was torn in two with the realization that Natalie and Kent were in the middle of the worst and most traumatic experience of their lives and I wasn't there to hold them, to dry their tears, to sing them to sleep.

Sleepyhead, it's time for bed.
I will sing to you until you're fast asleep.

Close your eyes, I won't go away.
Little one, the day is done.
I will hold you gently rocking to and fro
Singing soft this simple melody.

Hush my dear, your mother's near...
Oh how much I love your sleepy head....

From, Sleepyhead, Sheryl Nixon, 1984

Would they feel like I had deserted them? How could I be completely consumed with Reed and Robert, when Natalie and Kent desperately needed me as well?

Our two older daughters, Raelene, twenty, and Renae, nineteen, were attending college at Brigham Young University (BYU) in Provo, Utah, when they found out about the accident involving all of their siblings. Without our knowledge, our friends Charlene and Maury Hiers used their air miles to fly the girls home two days after the accident—an incredible gesture of kindness and love. After visiting Reed and Robert in the hospital, Raelene and Renae took care of Natalie and Kent at home while Mark and I spent our days and nights at the hospital with Reed and Robert.

I was so preoccupied with the boys those first few days that I didn't even think to call Natalie's or Kent's pediatricians. I came home one afternoon and found Natalie in excruciating pain. After realizing my mistake, I called her doctor. Unfortunately, the doctor was out of her office for two days with a death in her family, and Natalie didn't get in to see her until a week after the accident. Natalie's diagnosis was severe neck spasms. She had a CT scan and x-rays from her head to her tail bone and was immediately put on muscle relaxants. She began physical therapy a few days later.

Six days after the wreck, Kent had the stitches taken out of the wounds he'd received from the flying glass. The scratches down both sides of his face were gradually healing, and he looked much better. However, the knot on his forehead and the scars around his waist were permanent.

Reed remembers the first time Natalie came to visit him in the hospital. She looked tired and in pain as she stood by his door. Then she turned and left. Mark and I had told Natalie to take off her cervical collar and not to cry or upset Reed, but her neck hurt so much without the support of the collar that she had to leave to put it back on.

A few minutes later when Natalie returned, Reed looked over at her, and with tears in his eyes, mouthed the words, "I'm sorry."

Struggling to hold back her tears, she read Reed's lips (he was unable to speak since he was on life support) as he asked her about each of the kids in the accident. Natalie was surprised at Reed's concern for everyone else when he was hurt so badly himself. When she left the room she broke down, sobbing for her brother.

Two days after the accident, Reed and Robert both had metal halos surgically screwed into their skulls. The halos looked like big, wide, metal horseshoes. One end fastened with a metal screw a little behind one ear, the curved part crossing in front of their foreheads with a second and third screw above each eyebrow; it ended behind the other ear with a fourth screw.

Robert's halo was attached first, and fortunately he doesn't remember the procedure. When he was put back in bed, bags of water were hooked to his halo and hung down over the head of the bed, putting his neck in traction. The weight of the water would gradually pull on his neck, making room for his neck to align itself correctly. Within two days, Robert's neck was back in its proper position.

The same procedure was done on Reed, but his neck didn't move at all, and he was losing the little bit of movement he had. His neck would have to be stabilized some other way. The doctor told us Reed's fourth vertebra had broken into so many pieces that it needed to be surgically removed and replaced with bone either from Reed's thigh or from the hospital's bone bank. I had no idea there *was* such a thing as a bone bank! It seemed like we had to make one big decision after another; we felt so inadequate and unaware of what to do. We finally decided that, since Reed's body was already traumatized enough, another surgery would only add to his pain and suffering, so we would use bone from the hospital's bank.

I felt very uneducated trying to figure out all of the medical jargon the doctors used to explain things to me. It seemed like they spoke in code, and I didn't have the slightest idea what they were talking about. I eventually discovered that if I asked the doctors to draw pictures for me as they explained what they were doing, I could understand things well enough to tell our friends and family what was going on with Reed and Robert.

CHAPTER **5**

DURING THOSE FIRST days after the accident, family members came to help and support us. My mom, Donna, flew in from Switzerland, where she and my dad were serving a mission for our church. It was a relief to see her, and I really appreciated her coming from so far away. She arrived just in time to see Reed before he went in for surgery to stabilize his neck. She was able to stay only a few days, so after spending some time with Reed, Robert, and our family, she returned to Switzerland.

Mark's mother, Joyce, came from Milwaukee, Wisconsin where for nearly three years she and Mark's dad, Reed Sr., had been on a church assignment. Dad Nixon had been appointed as President over 170 full-time Latter-day Saint (LDS) missionaries and was unable to leave his responsibilities, but Mom Nixon took a leave of absence to come and help us.

I couldn't have made it through the next few weeks without her. She sat with Reed or Robert when I couldn't be there. Now each of my sons had one of us at his side each day, and if either boy needed me, Mom Nixon could come and get me. Before she came, I had been at my wits' end trying to monitor both boys at the same time. Because they were paralyzed, neither of them could press the nurse's call button, and they had to wait until someone came into their room to ask for help. I was terrified that they might have an "event" and no one would be there to save them. Every minute I was in one of the boys' rooms, half of my mind and heart was stretched toward the other room, fearing that my other son was in need.

Because Mom Nixon crocheted or read while she sat with her grandsons each day, Robert was worried that she might not notice if he needed something, since he couldn't move or speak. One time he clicked his tongue to get her attention. It worked! When Mom Nixon and I traded rooms, she told Reed how to let her know when he needed something, and the method caught on as the way for Reed and Robert to get people's attention.

Friday morning Reed was in the operating room (OR) where the doctors made an incision in the front of his neck to remove the fourth vertebra and replace it with bone from the hospital's bone bank. Then they fused the third, fourth, and fifth vertebra together with a metal plate, which stabilized his neck. It seemed strange, going through the front of Reed's neck to reach his spine. I thought there would be a lot more surgical trauma that way. I was also worried about people seeing the scar across Reed's throat. Worrying about something as trivial as a scar just showed how naïve I was in the beginning.

Before the surgery, Reed could shrug both of his shoulders and flex his right bicep a little bit. But even though surgery was the only way Reed's neck could support his head, Mark and I were so disappointed when, after the operation, Reed couldn't move or feel anything from the neck down. His initial injury was at the fourth cervical vertebrae (C4). As a result of the surgery removing the shattered bone and fusing the metal plate in place, the trauma to the area caused so much swelling that the nerves in Reed's spinal column were injured even more and caused Reed to function as a C1/C2 quadriplegic instead of a C4 quad. The higher the injury on the neck (C1 being the highest), the less function an individual will have.

When Reed awoke and found out that he couldn't move anything from his neck down, he wondered what had gone wrong during the surgery. He expected the operation to improve his situation, not make things worse. When he learned that nothing had gone wrong and that his loss of function was due to swelling, he hoped that as the swelling went down he'd regain the use of his bicep and shoulder shrug, but he was told that his loss might be permanent. Unfortunately Reed never regained any function. In fact, if he had, his whole rehabilitation would have been dramatically different. As it was, Reed couldn't hold his head up without support, his ability to swallow was severely weakened, and the possibility of eventually breathing on his own was no longer possible. Other problems manifested themselves as time went on.

At first, the doctors thought Robert's injuries were worse than Reed's, because Robert's neck was broken in three places and Reed's was broken in only one. But Robert had some sensation in his body and movement from his mid-chest up. He could move his arms, but not his hands. Reed's vertebra was shattered instead of being broken, so his injuries ended up being the more serious of the two.

After a week, the doctors discovered pressure building up on some nerves in Reed's neck, so they had to do another surgery. This time they operated from the back of Reed's neck, hoping to remove a fragment of bone they were unable to reach during the first operation, and release the pressure on his nerves at the same time.

During all of this Mark was torn up emotionally, but he didn't feel like he could share his inner struggle even with me, since I was having a hard time keeping it all together myself.

One particularly difficult day, he excused himself after lunch to take a walk alone while I waited in the hospital cafeteria. When he returned he was still miserable. Then we looked up and saw two of his brothers, Robert and Clair, walk into the cafeteria.

Mark really needed them right then, and the timing of their arrival was perfect. He was tremendously relieved to have two of his closest friends there with him at the hospital. He needed to share his internal pain and sorrow with someone other than me. Mark's brother Robert had been especially busy writing his dissertation at Texas A&M University, but flew to be with Mark when he heard of the accident. Clair's wife Laura had just delivered their tenth child the day before, but she said she'd be fine and encouraged Clair to "go be with Mark and Sheryl."

Because so many of our extended family were with us that first week, we frequently took advantage of the chance to pray together. It was a memorable bonding time for our families as we shared our faith and our love in sincere fasting and prayer. The strength we received from those prayers helped us endure the difficult days that followed.

CHAPTER **6**

AFTER MISSING A week of work, Mark needed to return to Bentley University. However, on the morning he was going to go back to work, we received a phone call from a nurse saying that Reed was in terrible pain and he had asked her to call us. This was supposed to be my first day at the hospital without Mark, and it had already begun with a problem.

When I arrived at the hospital I immediately asked for medication to soothe Reed's pain, but I was told that his doctor had to be consulted first. Why hadn't that been done before I got there? After a couple of hours waiting for the nurses to reach the doctor and trying to help Reed deal with his pain, I was frustrated to learn that the neurosurgeon couldn't be reached to authorize any medication. So now what? Praying for help, I watched Reed closely to see when his pain was the worst, hoping to discover what was causing the problem.

Both boys were put on special beds designed to reduce the risk of pneumonia and bed sores. The beds rotated from side to side, shifting their body weight to reduce the pressure points caused by being in bed day after day. Pressure weakened the skin and caused sores. These unique beds tilted until one side almost touched the floor and then reversed and tilted the other direction. After watching Reed for quite a while, I suddenly realized that every time his bed tilted, the weight of the metal halo made his head turn slightly, which caused him intense pain. After the surgery Reed's neck was stabilized, so I wondered why he still had to wear the halo. I was hoping that without it, his pain would ease up. Since pain medicine wasn't an option, I asked the nurse to at least stop the bed from tilting. After she did, Reed felt much better.

Later that evening as Reed's halo was removed, the doctor told him, "Oh, this shouldn't hurt. You won't feel a thing." But when he loosened the screws Reed felt and heard the cracking and grinding of his skull, and a tremendous pain and pressure built in his head, like a balloon ready to burst. Once the halo was gone, though, he was finally able to calm down and rest. I whispered a prayer of gratitude for the help the Lord had given me that day.

Two days later Robert went in for surgery on the back of his neck to relieve pressure on some of his nerves. The surgeon hoped that with the surgery he could restore some feeling and movement in Robert's left arm. At first Robert had a feeding tube going through his nose, down his throat, and into his stomach, as well as a chest tube helping him breathe. The tube down his nose and throat had been removed and Robert was able to eat, drink, and speak a little bit. However, during the surgery the doctor decided to put a trachea tube directly into Robert's trachea in the front of his neck to keep his left lung from collapsing. Without it, there was a forty percent chance that Robert could have another cardiac "event."

After the tracheal surgery, however, Robert couldn't eat, drink, or speak, and not being prepared for such a big setback, Robert became very discouraged. The very next day, however, he began to get some movement and feeling in his left arm, so the surgery had been a blessing.

A few days later I arrived at the hospital and learned that earlier that morning Reed's trachea tube had popped off. His ventilator alarm sounded and his breathing had stopped. The head nurse told me he was okay now and led me into her office to explain what had happened. Apparently, there was a patient in the room next to Reed's whose alarm kept going on and off randomly, so the nurses had become accustomed to the sound and were slow to react. When Reed's alarm went off, the nurses assumed it was the patient next door and didn't pay attention or respond immediately.

In the meantime, Reed lay in his bed, staring at the doorway, unable to move, unable to call out, desperate for air, his alarm ringing, but no one responding, searching for someone—anyone—to come and save him. Endless seconds ticked off the clock as he descended into a frightening, black unconsciousness. Disoriented, Reed was eventually drawn out of the deep darkness by echoing voices of panicked doctors and nurses calling out, "Reed, Reed, wake up! Come back to us!"

When Reed finally regained consciousness, he felt very strange and he couldn't move his lips at all. It was very scary for him because that was his only way of communicating. He was angry that the nurses weren't keeping a closer eye on him. At the nurses' front desk there was a monitor for each patient, so why wasn't someone watching? From that time forward, Reed's anxiety level was much higher. If he couldn't trust the doctors and nurses to watch out for him, whom could he trust?

When I found out about the pop-off I was livid! Reed was in the Intensive Care Unit, for heaven's sake. Where was his nurse—or any nurse, for that matter? Mark asked the doctor about oxygen deprivation and potential problems to Reed's already severely traumatized nervous system. The doctor said we wouldn't know the effect until sometime later.

Guilt encompassed me. I felt awful that I hadn't been at the hospital that morning to be with Reed. If I had been there, I could have made sure he was taken care of properly. But I had been at home getting the other kids off to school. I was overwhelmed with the realization that my sons needed me every minute of every day. There was no way I could physically, mentally, or emotionally fill that need. What do you do when you can't trust the medical personnel? How do you resolve it?

There was no simple answer. In fact, I still worry about Reed when he's in the hospital. I try to be with him as much as I can. Reed is never alone at home and we go to great lengths to keep him safe. In all the years of Mark's and my being in charge of Reed's care, Reed has never been unconscious due to a lack of air. We've had to sacrifice to make sure he always had the help he needed and was never left alone. However, we couldn't do it by ourselves; it's been a group effort. We have always had the help and support of our neighbors and friends.

After both Robert and Reed's brushes with death in the ICU, Mark and I realized that either of our sons could die at any moment. In fact, some people even encouraged us to "pull the plug" on the boys' life-support systems. We decided to be straightforward with Reed and Robert. We asked them individually whether they wanted us to do everything possible to keep them alive if a life or death decision was required in the future, or if they would rather be allowed to die. Though they couldn't speak, each of them let us know their feelings. "Of course I want to live! What do you think?" Both sons assured us they knew that the Lord still had purposes for their lives that He wanted fulfilled.

Even though Reed and Robert were so fragile that they could easily die, that obviously wasn't the plan, at least for now. The realization that Reed and Robert's lives were in God's hands and that He would take them from the Earth when He was ready—in His own time—gave us great strength and comfort.

It was that very night, Thursday, that we learned that the Prophet and President of The Church of Jesus Christ of Latter-day Saints (LDS), President Gordon B. Hinckley, would be coming to the hospital Saturday morning to visit Reed, Robert, and our family. President Hinckley had been named President of the LDS Church at a conference less than three weeks before, just two days before the accident. Despite the pressing responsibilities of his new assignment, President Hinckley felt that he should keep the speaking engagement he had previously been assigned in Massachusetts.

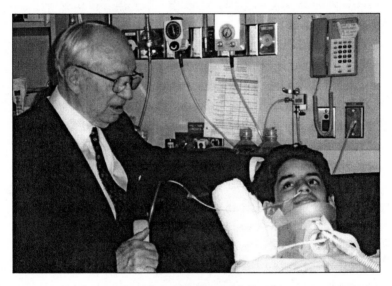

President Hinckley with Reed

We knew that hundreds, if not thousands, of prayers were being offered on behalf of our boys, and we could tell that these prayers were being answered. I knew with all of my heart and soul that through the power of God, Reed and Robert could be healed.

The night before President Hinckley's arrival, however,

four of Reed and Robert's cross-country friends came to visit Mark and me at the hospital. They told us that they wanted to hold some fundraisers to show their support for Reed and Robert and help with the ever-increasing medical bills we were facing. Their plans would include a 5K road race, a school dance, a banquet, and an auction. Those would be very ambitious projects to take on, we pointed out, and they agreed, but they exclaimed, "We know that with the help of our parents and others, we can do it!" They explained that there wasn't much else they could do, and they would be honored if we would allow them the opportunity to help their teammates and friends.

Mark and I were speechless. They wanted to do all of this for us? We had lived in Northborough only a year and a half, and aside from our neighbors and church friends, Mark and I didn't know very many people. But although Mark and I had yet to integrate into the community, Reed and Robert had already established themselves in the school and community, and were well-accepted. Reed and Robert's teammates and friends cared about them so much that they wanted to do all they could to help them. How could we turn down such a remarkable and generous offer? We couldn't.

While I was overwhelmed with gratitude at their desire to help us, I was dismayed with a sudden spiritual insight. As much as I didn't want to accept it, I knew in my heart that my sons would not be healed in the miraculous way I had hoped for. Oh, I still knew that the Lord had the power to heal them, but I could also see that many people's lives would be motivated to do good when they learned of Reed and Robert's circumstances.

I had such mixed emotions. It was all well and good that many people's lives would be blessed, but what about Reed and Robert's lives? And what about my own? Was it really necessary that we sacrifice so much? Unfortunately it wasn't our place to tell God that we didn't want this trial. In the end, however, He would bless us through countless acts by both friends and strangers. As these many people responded to the Lord's inspiration to show us support and love, their lives and ours would be blessed.

CHAPTER **7**

REED CONTINUED TO feel responsible for his injured siblings and friends who were in the accident. He often asked me how his friends were doing and if Natalie and Kent were okay. He seemed relieved to hear that they were all back in school. But Reed couldn't be comforted when it came to Robert. One day he asked me if I thought Robert was mad at him. I told him Robert hadn't said anything about being mad to me. I tried to reassure him, but Reed wouldn't let it go.

Finally, not knowing what else to do, I said, "Do you want me to ask Robert about it?"

I was surprised and nervous when Reed answered, "Yes."

How could I ask Robert such a sensitive and personal question? I decided that coming right out with it would be the best way, so I went to Robert's room and carefully said, "Reed is afraid you are mad at him because you are hurt so badly."

With a look of sadness and then almost anger, Robert pounded his arm on the bed and emphatically mouthed the words, "No! Why does he think that?"

I tried to explain, "Because you are Reed's brother and closest friend—he is afraid that the close relationship you have shared might be lost."

Robert assured me that he wasn't mad, and just felt more concern for his brother than he did for himself. I went back to Reed and assured him that Robert wasn't mad at him. Reed seemed very relieved, and the question never came up again.

As I mentioned before, neither Reed nor Robert was able

to speak, so we had to learn to read their lips. For some reason I could read Reed's lips much easier than I could Robert's. When I couldn't figure out what Robert tried to tell me, he got very frustrated. He'd been a straight-A student and was used to being in control, knowing what he wanted, and working hard to get it. But this having to rely on other people to read his lips and then guess what he wanted was a hard pill to swallow.

One time during that first week, Robert tried to tell me something that I didn't understand, so I asked him to repeat it. When I couldn't quite catch it the second time and asked him to say it yet again, he pounded his arm on the bed with frustration and mouthed the words, "Never mind!"

I felt terrible that I couldn't understand what he needed and wanted. But what could I do? I empathized with him, realizing that when I spoke to my kids when they were little, I always expected a quick answer, never "What did you say?"

To me, Robert seemed like a young child—alone and afraid. Many times in the hospital Robert felt anxious and distressed to the point that he asked me to sing to him. It calmed him down only for a few moments, and then he was upset again. One morning while I was in Robert's room, he told me he was afraid of a big bear on his stomach and begged me to get it off. He told me to "come closer, closer, closer—now put your arms out—grab him! Now get rid of him!" I made the motions as if I were snatching the imaginary bear off Robert's stomach and heaving it away. Even though it felt very strange to me, Robert did feel better after that.

After leaving his room, I asked the nurse what was going on with Robert. When she told me that he was on pain medication that sometimes caused hallucinations, I asked her to contact his doctor immediately and discontinue the medicine.

I was very surprised that the nurses seemed unconcerned with the hallucinations, since they were making Robert so frightened. I told her to find something else to help him with the pain. Leaving him terrified seemed unacceptably cruel.

After two weeks, Reed and Robert were stable enough for us to begin making arrangements to move them to a rehabilitation hospital. But which one? We didn't know a thing about rehab hospitals, and we had no idea how to find one. UMASS provided us with a list of rehab facilities across the country. There were many great places for rehabilitation, but with Natalie and Kent still at home, I couldn't possibly leave for five months. We decided that we had to find a place in Massachusetts.

By that time, Robert was well enough to start the gradual process of weaning off the ventilator, gradually breathing for himself a little longer each day. With Robert no longer vent-dependent, we found quite a few places for him to rehabilitate, but Reed was still on the vent. With his condition so critical and demanding, we couldn't find a single place that would accept him.

Besides, there was no way I could possibly take care of both Reed and Robert in two separate hospitals. We just *had* to find a rehab facility that would take both of them. Finally UMASS told us that they might have found a place where both Reed and Robert could go, the Veteran's Administration Hospital (VA) in West Roxbury, about an hour from our home. Although neither of our sons had been in the military, the VA doctors were well-trained and had a lot of experience with spinal cord injuries (SCI) from the many wounded soldiers sent there. It was by far the best place for our sons to go, so UMASS made the arrangements. After three weeks in the PICU, Robert was moved to the VA Rehabilitation Hospital, with Reed following a week later. Two critical cases in the same hospital in the same week would be too much, even for the VA.

Robert could speak a little bit by then, but the process to get Reed speaking again was much more complicated and would have to come later. When Mark told Reed that Robert could speak *and* breathe on his own, Reed mouthed the words, "Well, what did he do? How did he do it? I'll do whatever it takes if you just tell me what to do!" Mark's heart broke as he explained to Reed that there wasn't anything he could do. Reed's injury was right where all of the nerves to his breathing muscles connected to the spinal cord. As a result, he would probably never be able to breathe on his own again; he would be vent-dependent for the rest of his life.

Reed was very disappointed. He had thought that with therapy and rehab he would regain some sensation and function, and that he just needed to work really hard to get better. He didn't view it any differently than other injuries he'd had to that point in his life. As time went on, Reed still hoped and expected to get better, but he began to realize it was going to take a lot longer than he'd initially thought.

CHAPTER **8**

REED AND ROBERT had been in the VA Hospital for two weeks when Mark and I were asked to attend a meeting with all of the doctors, nurses, and other medical staff involved in our sons' care. Apparently, the medical personnel were concerned that Mark and I had unrealistic expectations for the future and that we hadn't fully understood the realities of our sons' injuries, so they thought they'd better speak to us about it.

It was true that we had heavy, but hopeful hearts. We had heard many doctors say that there was a possibility that Reed and Robert's nerves could repair themselves and function again, even up to two years after they were damaged. Reed was hoping to be able to serve a two-year mission for our church when he turned nineteen, and we were encouraging him in that direction. He was willing and even determined to cooperate and work hard in his rehab program so he could reach that goal. He often said, "Just tell me what to do and I'll do it!"

So the medical staff thought they needed to meet with us to help us learn what to expect, what physical limitations the boys would have, and what we should anticipate when Reed and Robert were finally able to come home.

The doctors told us that over the next couple of years they expected Robert, with some help, to be able to feed himself, dress himself, and maybe even drive a car. He could learn to be self-sufficient. We were so happy and relieved that, although different, his life could still be enjoyable. But when the doctors told us what to expect for Reed, we almost lost all hope. They didn't expect any recovery for him at all. He would never be able to walk, to feed himself, to drive, or do anything we had hoped would be possible. I blinked as Mark and I looked at each other. We were devastated.

With Mother's Day approaching and Reed unable to buy me a card, he asked one of the nurses to get a nice card at the hospital's gift shop and sign it for him. After reading that touching card, I looked up and Reed mouthed the words, "Next year I'll sign it myself."

I guess we all had unrealistic hopes for the future.

The truth was that Reed could never again be left alone; he wouldn't have any privacy for the rest of his life. There would always be a nurse, a personal care attendant (PCA), or a family member with him. He would need help in every aspect of his life, in every single thing he ever did. The closest thing to privacy he would ever have would be when we listened for him on a monitor during the night just in case he clicked his tongue to get our attention.

I had realized that this was going to be a long road and that there would be a lot of things Reed would miss out on, but I had never thought his condition would be so limiting and serious—forever. There would never be a light at the end of the tunnel. Mark and I cried through the whole meeting. When it was over, the head nurse invited me to use her office to take as much time as I needed to pull myself together.

I bawled and wailed, grieving for my sons—and for me. I knew that all of the pressure and responsibility for their care and well-being would be on *my* shoulders, and I didn't know how I would ever be able to handle two disabled sons at home relying completely on me. Not only would Reed and

Robert require my help, but Natalie and Kent were still young and would also need me. With poor health myself, I couldn't imagine any way to get through it.

Allowing myself to break down emotionally, even for one day, would set me back physically, emotionally, and spiritually. I would be exhausted, bone-tired, unable to think straight, and lack the will to do anything but stay in bed and wallow in the depths of despair.

> ...When you're out of control with no help in sight
> And you just wanna quit, but you know it's not right...
> Just to give up the fight and lie there in bed....
> *From, Look Inward, Sheryl Nixon, 1996*

I would finally have to increase my depression medication to pull myself out of that dark hole. I was convinced that spending precious energy grieving would only make things worse. I learned that if I let my emotions become extreme, whether I was excited, happy, angry, or sad, my depression and fibromyalgia would flare up and I would physically pay for the emotional spree for days, if not weeks. The doctors had never told me about this, so I went through it over and over again until, through trial and error, I finally figured it out. I found myself thanking God for medicine that made it possible for me to function somewhat normally.

There in the nurse's office I knew that if I didn't take control of my emotions right then, I wouldn't have the strength to deal with the difficult challenges I was facing. So...I dried my tears and put my faith and trust in God to help me through one day at a time. There was work to be done.

➤➤➤

Those many months with Reed and Robert in the hospital were so crammed with details and slow progress that I'm sure I wouldn't have remembered as much about the accident and the years that followed if I hadn't kept a journal. I spent so much time at the hospital with Reed and Robert that I had plenty of time to reflect and write.

I started keeping a journal when I was a child, but I wrote only on Sundays when all of my family gathered to write in their individual journals. As I got older, I didn't write very often until I had graduated from high school and begun my singing career. I was a freshman at Brigham Young University (BYU) when I auditioned for a performing group on campus, The Sounds of Freedom. I made the cut, and in 1971 I toured the Northwestern United States with them, singing and performing. That's when I bought a journal and wrote about the performances on my first tour.

Unfortunately, taking a load of college courses, working part-time, and practicing and performing with The Sounds of Freedom took their toll on me. I got sick and was hospitalized for a week and had to drop out of college. In the spring of 1972, though, I auditioned and was accepted to go on a twenty-day tour to Vietnam with the United Services Organizations (a department of the Army more commonly known as the USO) where I sang and performed for the soldiers. Later that same year, I joined another USO show for a six-week tour in eight European countries. During those two overseas tours, I wrote all of the details in my journal.

All around the world, doesn't matter where you go,
There's people singin' in the shower or with the radio.
Everyone loves music, whether rock or lullaby.
I'm no different from the rest. Music gets me high.

Cause more than anything, oh more than anything,
More than anything, I love to sing.

From, I Love To Sing, Sheryl Nixon, 1986

It wasn't until the following summer, when I was twenty years old, that I decided to start keeping a daily journal. Only three days later, at a parking lot dance for my apartment complex, I met my future husband. That night I wrote in my journal, "I danced the last four or five dances with a cute guy named Mark Nixon. He's a very good dancer... and I wouldn't mind getting to know him a little better." We were married one year later. After that year of journal writing I decided to continue writing, although less often, and now I have fifteen volumes of journals written over the past thirty-seven years.

1974 Mark & Sheryl's wedding reception

Until after the accident, I had never really thought about writing in a journal as anything more than just keeping track of the ups and downs of everyday life. I never imagined that my journal writing would end up being a window into my heart and soul, transcribing my feelings and emotions on paper as I wandered down the unknown path that was to become my future.

CHAPTER 9

ALTHOUGH REED COULDN'T breathe without the ventilator, there were some things he could work on to improve his quality of life, such as relearning to swallow, eat, and speak. At first Reed wasn't allowed to eat anything by mouth because his body was still being stabilized. For almost a month he was fed liquids from a long tube that went through his nose, down his throat, and into his stomach. (See picture on page 33) One day a nurse accidentally tripped on the tube, ripping it out of Reed's stomach and halfway out his throat, so a new tube had to be put in. Not only was it painful to insert the new tube, but Reed hated the taste of the numbing ointment the doctor used when replacing it.

The very next day *that* tube somehow got clogged and had to be taken out. A resident doctor put another tube through Reed's nose and down his throat and then took an x-ray to make sure it was in the right position. The x-ray showed that the tube wasn't down far enough to reach Reed's stomach, so the doctor took it out and tried again, but it still wasn't right. He tried over and over, but the tube kept curling and coming out of Reed's mouth. Finally after trying *eight* more times, the doctor gave up and decided that someone else would have to replace the feeding tube the next day. By then it was 1:30 in the morning. We were all very exhausted and frustrated, and Mark and I still had an hour's drive home.

Earlier that same day we were told that Reed needed

a gastric feeding tube, or G-tube, because if his nose tube stayed in much longer than three weeks scar tissue would start building up on his larynx. Instead of going through Reed's nose and throat, the G-tube would go through his abdomen directly into his stomach. That way he could get all of his food, liquids, and medications without having to swallow.

The G-tube was scheduled to be put in four days later, but after all of the problems we'd had the night before we decided not to wait. Mark was at the hospital bright and early the next morning to make sure that no one put another nose tube in only to take it out again a few days later. Reed really appreciated his dad making sure the G-tube got put in that very afternoon because he felt so much better without the tube in his nose. When Reed was finally able to swallow, eat, and drink enough to maintain good health on his own, the G-tube would be removed.

Reed had a lot of tests run before he could eat anything through his mouth. It was important to make sure the food went down his throat into his stomach and not into his lungs. Everyone has a natural reflex that makes sure that only food goes down the esophagus and only air goes down the trachea. Reed no longer had that reflex.

The damage to Reed's neck and nerves made it hard to swallow. His saliva, which he normally would have swallowed without even thinking about it, pooled at the back of his throat. To get the saliva out, he had to spit into a cup all day long. Since swallowing lubricates your throat, Reed's throat was very dry, making it even harder to learn to swallow normally.

One of the tests showed that Reed didn't have enough control over his muscles to swallow correctly. This forced him to have to swallow three or four times just to get one bite of food down. Swallowing liquids was even harder.

The first time Reed tried to eat, he was fed a bite of ice cream. However, most of the ice cream came out of the hole in his neck where his trachea tube had been put in. Because he was a silent aspirator (couldn't feel the food go into his windpipe), we wouldn't know if he had accidentally swallowed food into his lungs. Able-bodied people would feel the food and either cough to get it out or choke.

An ear, nose, and throat (ENT) doctor came to help Reed relearn to swallow. To begin with, the ENT used strained foods and colored each one with a different color of special dye. After feeding Reed each color of the pureed food, the ENT took x-rays to make sure the food went down through Reed's esophagus and not his windpipe. Any food going into Reed's lungs could cause pneumonia or even death from blocking off his air supply.

A device on Reed's trachea tube called a cuff was designed like a balloon to be inflated or deflated. If the cuff was inflated, food couldn't accidentally go into his lungs. However, an inflated cuff also prevented air from going over his vocal cords, not allowing him to speak. On May 12 Reed's cuff was deflated for the first time and air passed over his vocal cords. After five weeks of reading lips, I finally heard Reed's first words: "It's nice to be able to talk again!"

Oh, the magic and the beauty of the human voice! Hearing Reed speak again was like a thunderstorm of emotions, soaking me clear through to the skin. A voice never sounded as wonderful to me as Reed's did at that moment!

Speaking with a ventilator is totally different from normal talking. People usually inhale, filling their lungs with air, and then they talk as they exhale and the air passes the vocal cords on its way out. But the only time air passed Reed's vocal cords was when the ventilator gave him a breath—inhaling for him. He had to learn to speak while inhaling instead of exhaling, which was completely opposite of what he used to do naturally. The inhale from the ventilator only lasted two seconds. Reed had to learn the timing of the ventilator just perfect in order to get as many words out in one breath as possible. If he missed the timing he could only speak one or two words. A speech therapist helped Reed begin the long, drawn-out process of reversing his speaking habits.

The therapist had Reed practice speaking by saying the days of the week as fast as he could in one breath. He got through Thursday. When I tried this myself I was able to say the days of the week six times in one breath! Then the therapist asked him to count to twenty-one to see how many breaths it took him. It took four, with a little to spare. In one breath I counted to seventy! I could see right off that progress was going to be really slow. After that, the therapist inflated Reed's cuff. That was enough for one day.

Gradually Reed was able to tolerate the cuff being deflated for longer periods of time until he could speak all day long. At night though, his cuff had to be inflated to avoid any possible problems while he slept. If Reed needed anything at night, he would have to click his tongue and someone would come to help him, but sometimes the nurse who came wasn't very helpful.

One night Reed woke up feeling short of breath and clicked for the nurse to AMBU (Ambulatory Manual Breathing Unit) bag him to give him extra breaths.

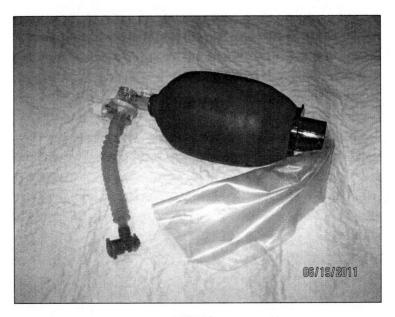

06/19/2011

AMBU bag

She told him to wait a few minutes and "let the ventilator work for you." When Reed continued to feel uncomfortable and asked her again, she refused and said, "You just need to calm down." After several more requests for help she still refused, saying, "Someday you'll thank me for not helping you." Reed thought to himself, "Who is she? I need help, not a trainer or coach!" After she left the room, Reed clicked once again for help and a different nurse came and gave him the extra breaths he needed.

It was a slow process, but Reed gradually learned to speak clearer and stronger. However, he could speak only when the ventilator gave him air, so he'd say four or five words and then he would be out of breath. He had to wait about four seconds for the ventilator to give him more air before he could continue. Having to wait really broke up his speaking. It's amazing how long four seconds can feel when you're waiting for the rest of a sentence. Sometimes the silence made people so nervous that they started talking again without realizing that Reed hadn't finished what he was saying. Even though he could speak, speaking was very different than it had been before the accident.

Speaking connects people throughout the world in everything from their daily conversations to their employment and social interactions. Mark and I knew we had to do everything possible to make sure Reed's voice was strong and clear, because speaking was one of the very few things he actually *could* do.

CHAPTER **10**

WHILE REED WAS working on relearning to eat and speak, Robert was dealing with his own problems. He had already had his trachea tube removed, but unlike Reed, Robert's halo was still screwed into his skull. Not only did Robert have to continue wearing the halo, but before getting to the VA Hospital, metal rods had been added and connected to a sheepskin vest he had to wear. The whole contraption kept his head, neck, and body in one position until his broken neck bones healed.

Robert was about six feet tall and weighed 120 pounds: he was pretty thin. The vest and metal rods were right next to his body, and other than the thin layer of sheepskin, there wasn't any padding. Bit by bit the rods rubbed against Robert's skin and shoulder blade bones until he began complaining of terrible back pain. He constantly asked me—or anyone else around—to rub his back. "Rub hard. Harder," he would plead. The vest was very tight against Robert's skin, so it was really difficult to rub hard enough to ease his pain.

Finally Robert's back hurt so much that the VA doctor sent him back to UMASS, where the vest was first put on, to see what should be done. Robert was gone all day and came back to the VA very disappointed. His UMASS doctor had said, "Well, simply putting Robert on his stomach will solve the problem."

We were shocked and surprised at his ridiculous solution. In the first place, it would be next to impossible to get Robert onto his stomach, but even if we could, not only would his nose practically touch the bed, he would be in a terribly awkward and uncomfortable position. Robert's VA doctor decided that from then on he would just have to do what he thought best.

The situation was made worse by muscle spasms (sudden involuntary contractions of one or more muscles). When a person cuts their finger it seems like the cut throbs right along with their heart beat. When Robert had spasms, the unbearable pain throbbed right where the rods had rubbed through the skin on his back. He tried to be patient, but when he couldn't handle it any longer he'd hit the nurse's call button with his arm, begging for pain medicine. Then the nurse had to call the doctor to authorize something strong enough for the pain. By the time the doctor got back to her, the medication got ordered, and administered, Robert was in so much agony that the pills barely helped at all. It was a never-ending battle.

Since I wasn't able to be at the hospital for my sons every minute of every day and night, I asked them what the nurses were like when I wasn't there. Robert told me that his day nurses were pretty good, but his night nurses were very impatient with him. He was in so much pain most of the time that he frequently hit the nurse's call button with his arm to ask for more pain medication. One particular night Robert's nurse got so tired of her call button going off that she went into Robert's room and said, "Don't hit that call button again unless you can't breathe!"

I felt anxious each night as I left the hospital, wondering if my sons would be neglected while I wasn't there. I was torn between wanting to be at the hospital and wanting to be at home. One half of me wished I could be with Reed and Robert every minute of every day and night to ease their suffering, but the other half of me longed for home where I could love and help Natalie and Kent. I just couldn't be in two places at the same time.

When I was at the hospital I spent a lot of time rubbing Robert's neck and shoulders, trying to relieve his suffering. One evening his pain was particularly bad. I spent four hours with him trying to help him relax and calm down, but nothing helped. I was heartbroken. I felt as though it was my responsibility to make everything better for my son, and all I could do was sit there, hold his hand, and cry with him. I could have allowed myself to drift back into that bottomless pit of depression, but my past experiences reminded me not to go there, even for a moment.

In spite of his pain, Robert made progress. One morning I arrived at the hospital and found the nurses helping him slowly sit up in bed: the first step in the process of getting him into a wheelchair. After lying in bed for a month, Robert couldn't sit up without getting dizzy. The nurses gradually raised the head of Robert's hospital bed a little at a time, day after day, until he could sit straight up and not get too lightheaded. Then they transferred him onto a bed that could transform into a chair. The head of the bed was slowly raised up while the foot was simultaneously lowered until Robert was sitting straight up. He couldn't stay in the sitting position very long because he got too dizzy.

Robert frequently repeated the sitting process, sitting in the chair a little longer each day, until he could finally sit in a real wheelchair. The first time he got into the wheelchair I pushed him to the gift shop, the cafeteria, and around the hospital grounds for a total of two and a half hours. When we returned to Robert's room, the nurses were all so proud of him. They told us that most patients were able to sit up for only half an hour before having to get back into bed. That put a huge smile on Robert's face. After that he got up in his wheelchair almost every day.

The last step in the sitting process was for Robert to learn to push the wheelchair himself. He was put into a special wheelchair that had knobs every six inches around the outside of each wheel. The nurse put a special pair of gloves (called push gloves) on Robert, with the palm of the glove covered in a hard rubber material. Since Robert's hands were paralyzed, these gloves helped him push against the knobs on the wheels and slowly move his chair forward with the little strength he had in his wrists and arms.

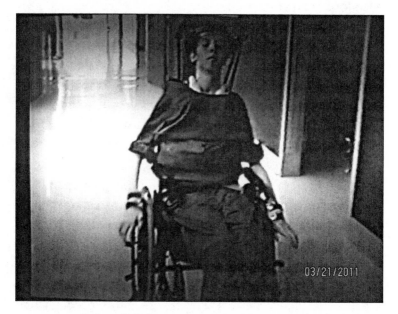

03/21/2011

Robert in halo & vest pushing his wheelchair

Robert's right arm was stronger and could push harder

than his left arm, so when he first tried to push his own chair he went in circles. It was kind of funny and yet heart-wrenching to watch him push himself around and around.

Robert worked very hard to strengthen his left arm. Before we knew it, he was pushing himself down the hall to visit Reed. Except for two brief moments, they hadn't seen each other for six weeks. Now they had a chance to talk for the first time since the accident. Robert pushed himself down to Reed's room nearly every day after that. These brothers and best friends who had spent most of their lives together could finally be together again. And Reed could see for himself that Robert still loved him and had no hard feelings about the accident.

We're in this together, together forever,
Together 'til the end of time.
Through stormy weather, hangin' in there together,
Somehow it'll turn out fine.
Well, I'll be here to help you through the hard times.
I'll be here in the good times, too.
Hey, we're gonna make it.
Nothin's gonna break it.
Together baby me an' you.

From, Together Forever, Sheryl Nixon, 1986

It was hard for Robert to visit Reed that first time when he actually understood the magnitude of Reed's injuries. He felt somewhat guilty that Reed had been hurt so much worse than he had. But they were so happy to be together again that they looked forward to their visits each day.

I was overjoyed that Reed and Robert could be together again. As unbelievable as it was to have two paralyzed sons,

I could see that they were a tremendous help and support to each other. They lifted each other's spirits and encouraged one another. They could sympathize with each other because they were the only ones who actually knew what the other one was going through. From then on I no longer had to carry messages back and forth from one room to another.

CHAPTER **11**

FOR AT LEAST three months after our children's accident, we were overwhelmed with newspaper and TV reporters. No one had ever heard of two SCI quadriplegic siblings, let alone their being injured in the same accident. This seemed incomprehensible to every person who heard of our circumstances. It took an incredible amount of time and energy for us to accommodate all of the media requests.

Many times I found out about an interview only an hour or two before it was supposed to take place. Sometimes the interviews were as simple as a reporter taking notes while speaking with us, but other interviews were much more involved, with sound and cameras, taping a segment to be shown that evening on the 6:00 and 11:00 news. During those times I felt like a cattle rancher in a mad dash, rounding everyone up from work and school to get them home in less than an hour. Still other times when I arrived at the hospital, reporters were already there waiting to interview and film us. It was usually hectic and chaotic trying to keep the media happy.

Months later, a friend of ours told us she had recently spoken with a news reporter who had been at the scene of our children's accident back in April. The reporter had seen many accidents with people frantically running around screaming, but when she arrived at the scene of Reed and Robert's accident, she "felt a sense of peace and calm that was remarkable and unique—almost tangible, even." Then, a couple of months later, she went to the hospital to interview the boys. She expected to find us all depressed and upset and the boys mentally and emotionally wiped out. But when she got to the hospital and saw Reed and Robert, there sat two teenage boys who *looked and acted* like teenagers even though their bodies didn't work like they had before their accident.

Reed in VA using hospital's wheelchair with sip and puff controls

She interviewed the boys and our family and told our friend, "Everyone was laughing, joking, and had high spirits and strong faith. I could not believe the experience I had in talking to the boys. I actually saw a glow around them." She felt such a wonderful spirit that she didn't want to leave, and said that it was one of the most remarkable interviews of her entire career as a reporter.

Over Memorial Day weekend, seven weeks after the accident, I was at the hospital with Reed and Robert when we saw the news report on television that Christopher Reeve had been thrown from his horse during an equestrian competition and had broken his neck. In a single moment he had become a quadriplegic on a ventilator. We just stared at the TV in shock. We knew exactly what his family and friends were going through and we were heartsick for them. I wrote Christopher Reeve a letter from our family expressing our sincere sympathy.

Christopher Reeve's spinal cord injury (SCI) was very similar to Reed's injury, except Reed's spinal cord had been torn clear through while Christopher Reeve's was only partially torn, giving Reeve a better chance to breathe on his own again. As sad as I was about Christopher Reeve's condition, I knew that because of it there would be widespread attention brought to spinal cord injuries and paralysis in general. Christopher and Dana Reeve were courageous in their determination that through their experiences they would help others with similar injuries.

Later on, Reed and Robert were interviewed for *The Today Show* with Katie Couric. The four-day series about spinal cord injuries ran in December 1995 with Christopher Reeve as the main guest. Reed and Robert were featured in a taped interview explaining the challenges and blessings they were experiencing.

Years later when I learned of Christopher Reeve's death, I wept all day long. Reed and Robert were sorry to hear of his passing, but it didn't overwhelm them like it had me. That evening I wondered why the news had affected me so much; I lay in bed that night pondering the question.

After some sincere soul searching, I discovered that without my realizing it, I had focused all of my hope for better lives for Reed and Robert on Christopher Reeve's life and the progress he made. After all, he was famous. I assumed that he had an unlimited supply of resources available to him. I subconsciously thought that as long as he was alive, my sons would live as well. It wasn't very rational thinking, but that's what I thought nonetheless. I knew Christopher Reeve would pave the way for Reed, Robert, and our family. What would we ever do now that he was gone?

Before falling asleep that night, I prayed for help remembering that Reed and Robert's lives were in God's hands. He knew of our struggles, our sadness, and our needs, so I just needed to renew my faith and trust in Him. I thanked God for Christopher Reeve's life. From the day of his accident in May of 1995 until he died in October of 2004, Christopher Reeve was a powerful voice, a well-known figure in promoting research, and a hope and inspiration to people with spinal cord injuries, as well as all disabled people.

CHAPTER **12**

IN JUNE MARK and I learned about an "Abilities Fair" at the World Trade Center in Boston and decided to go check it out. Before going inside, Mark and I talked about how negative the event would probably be, recognizing that we were a little uncomfortable around handicapped people, not always knowing how to act appropriately. We began to understand how other people might feel when they saw our sons. It made us sad to realize how far we, as well as society as a whole, still had to go in accepting disabled people in our communities.

We were at the Abilities Fair almost all day, looking at all sorts of tools, devices, computer adaptations, and van conversions, and learning about equipment vendors, rehabilitation centers, and information for help groups. If it hadn't been so personal for us, it would have been a very interesting adventure, but realizing that we were there for our own sons and knowing that they would be using many of these devices made the day very sad for us. People working at the fair were shocked when we told them why we were there. None of them had ever heard of circumstances like ours.

There were countless items to choose from such as wheelchairs, bathroom equipment, and computer environmental control units, just to name a few, and we had way too many decisions to make. Almost every item we looked at cost $20,000 or more.

We saw several different kinds of wheelchair controls: sip and puff units, joysticks that worked by moving the chin, voice-activated software, and a retainer-type system that fit in the roof of the mouth and was controlled with the tongue. We decided to get the New Abilities Tongue Touch Keypad (TTK) system, so that Reed wouldn't always have a straw-looking thing in front of his face, which would be required with the sip and puff wheelchair control (see picture on page 60). Besides, if the straw accidentally got moved out of reach, Reed would be stuck.

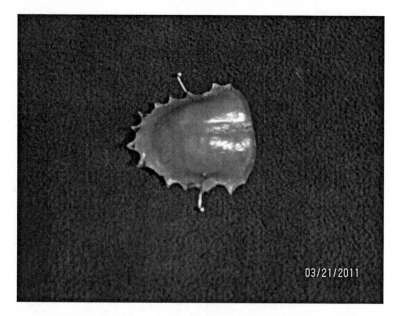

03/21/2011

TTK

Although the whole experience at the Abilities Fair was much more intense than we had imagined, we were able to make some very worthwhile decisions.

After spending the day at the World Trade Center, Mark and I went back to the hospital to visit Reed and Robert and tell them what we had learned. When we went into Robert's room, we were totally surprised and happy to see his vest and metal rods were gone! Robert's smile said it all. His halo was still there, but only until the doctors made sure that his neck would stay in place.

With the vest and rods gone we were able to see the sores on Robert's back. They weren't sores; they were deep wounds! Many times we'd tried to stuff foam padding down between the rods and Robert's back, but there just wasn't enough room. No wonder he'd been in so much pain! The metal rods had rubbed against his skin and bone for so long that we could actually see the muscle in one wound. The larger, deeper wound was the size of a golf ball, and we could see clear down to the bone. The damage was so much worse than we had ever thought. We realized that it would take a long time for the wounds to heal, but at least now they could heal. That night Robert's back touched the sheets for the first time in over two months.

Although the boys were progressing, there were still days when we were filled with such intense pain and heartache that we weren't sure we could make it through.

A few days after Robert's vest was removed, I arrived at the hospital and found him vomiting. The doctor had put Robert on some medicine to stop the calcium in his bones from sloughing off into his blood stream, a result of Robert's bones no longer bearing weight. Decalcification of his bones could cause seizures and kidney stones. I had previously learned that Robert was very sensitive to medications and now he was becoming sick from the side effects of this new medicine. Besides struggling with dry heaves and vomiting, Robert suddenly broke out into hives and swelling. I couldn't even touch him without his crying out in pain. He was miserable, and so was I.

And if all of that wasn't bad enough, at the same time, the

IV tube in Robert's left wrist hurt so much that they had to take it out and put in a new one—more pain. He hurt everywhere. Exhausted, he would doze off for a few minutes only to wake up to vomit again. He cried and cried. I spent the next four hours holding a pan for him each time he threw up, drying his tears, and trying to find some way to comfort him, as well as myself. As I sat there I wrote these words in an effort to calm my spirit.

> I remember the day when our lives turned gray,
> And the world we knew fell apart.
> I sat by your bed, thoughts raced through my head,
> A deep, aching throb filled my heart.
>
> You would not be the same as you ever had been.
> We would try to accept that now
> And pull what strength was inside us
> To learn how to cope somehow.
>
> As weeks go by, it's hard not to cry,
> But we work to get through each day.
> When we feel all alone in our twilight zone,
> We remember the need to pray.
>
> We open our hearts to the Lord, Jesus Christ
> And pray for strength through Him.
> Then work like it all depends on us
> But pray like it depends on Him.
>
> *Sheryl Nixon, 1995*

When I began writing those words, I was hoping to put the lyrics to a song I had begun writing a year before the accident entitled, "You Shall Have Peace in Me." I had written the words and music to the chorus, but I couldn't come up with a melody or lyrics for the verses. Several times I put the song aside because I wasn't making any progress. The words I'd just written while sitting with Robert created a heartfelt poem, but they didn't work for my song either.

There were countless times in past years when music and lyrics had come together for me right when I needed courage and strength during difficult days. Through the spiritual connection I felt with my music I was enabled to make it through those hard times.

But now I really struggled. There were no words in my heart or my head for the song of peace that I desperately needed to get through my harrowing journey. At that moment I intensely missed the spiritual connection I had felt from my music. Where would my comfort come from, if not through music? I longed for the peace this song could bring, but it wouldn't come. I wondered if it would *ever* come: the peace *or* the song.

I spent the evening with Robert while Mark was in with Reed, who was recovering from two surgical procedures: one to fix a collapsed lung, and the other to have his trachea tube changed. A size eight trachea tube was taken out, but the surgeon couldn't get a size eight back in. After ten tries, he decided to put a size seven in instead. By that time Reed was bruised, and his throat really hurt for the rest of the day. That night Mark tried to encourage him, "This was a bad day, Reed, just a bad day. Not all days will be bad like this one."

At one o'clock in the morning Mark and I left the hospital discouraged. With tears in his eyes Mark said, "I don't know when this is going to get easier. I guess it will get easier when the boys start feeling better. I hope it gets better in a hurry."

A week later after finishing our evening prayers with Reed, Mark and I headed off to Robert's room, but just as I was leaving I noticed that Reed's spirits were especially low, so I asked him why. He mouthed the words to me, "I'm tired of not being able to move."

I felt like I'd just been punched in the stomach. I didn't know how to respond. This was the first time I'd heard Reed complain, and I wasn't prepared. I asked if he wanted me to go get his dad so we could talk and he mouthed, "Yes, but have prayers with Robert first and then come back in to talk."

When Mark and I returned, Reed told us that he expected to be well in two years. When we asked him what made him think that, he said that in two years he would be nineteen and he thought he would be healed by then so he could go on his two-year mission for the Church. With no answer and little hope, Mark's eyes filled with tears as he assured Reed that, however long it took, he would be there for him. Mark told Reed that whatever ability Reed had now or in the future, *he must maximize it*. We would all be happy and thankful with any progress he made, but we needed to focus on maximizing the positive. From that moment on "maximization" became our family's motto.

During the days ahead, Robert worked to improve the function that he had by learning to use his wrist movement to close his fingers around various objects, such as a ball or a wooden block. He practiced picking the objects up out of a box and putting them on a table. After all of the objects were on the table, he picked each one up again and returned it to the box. I was surprised at how long it took to do such a simple task and how worn out Robert was by the time he'd finished.

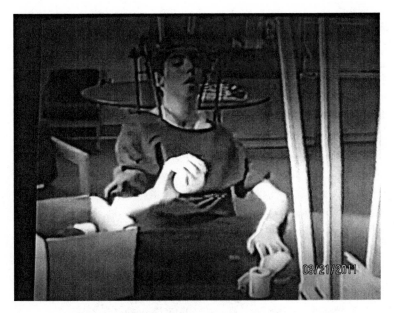

Robert picking up objects

Reed also worked to make progress, but instead of using his body he worked on his speech. By the end of May, Reed's cuff could be deflated for four hours at a time. After a few months he could speak all day long. We loved listening to him talk as much as he loved talking.

By this time, I had been away from home almost every day for two months. It was starting to take its toll. I was exhausted and had a hard time finding time to catch up on things I had put off at home, like paying bills, filling out medical paperwork, and running errands. I was also behind on a business I had begun back in 1987: singing, recording, and mailing "thank you" cassette tapes for car dealerships around the country.

But I especially missed being home for Natalie and Kent. Their lives were moving ahead, and most of the time I wasn't even there. Raelene and Renae did a great job keeping the housework up and taking care of Natalie and Kent, but it's hard to replace a mother. Raelene and Renae both would return to BYU in the fall when the boys came home, and I would be around for Natalie and Kent a little more, but I had no idea how busy I would be just taking care of Reed and Robert.

Besides being seen by their pediatricians, our insurance company required Natalie and Kent to be evaluated by a doctor that their company provided. I was completely caught off guard when the company's doctor informed me that nothing was wrong with either Natalie or Kent. I couldn't believe it! Kent had a huge hematoma or bump on his forehead, and Natalie continued to be in severe pain, barely functioning. But according to the insurance company's doctor she was "just fine." Ridiculous! I finally had to get letters written by Natalie's and Kent's physicians detailing each of their injuries to submit to the insurance company to verify that they really did have injuries resulting from the accident and that the insurance company was responsible to pay their medical bills.

Natalie was finally diagnosed with post-traumatic stress syndrome, post-traumatic headache disorder, depression, and fibromyalgia. She was still struggling as a result of the accident. She had nightmares and was afraid to drive in the car. She always asked the driver to "go slower."

Most of the time I spent with Natalie was at doctors' appointments, but I do remember leaving the hospital early one afternoon to participate with her in a mother/daughter basketball game and dinner.

Because Natalie and Kent were in school, it was hard to get them to the hospital to visit Reed and Robert. During the week they worried about their brothers and always asked how they were doing. I felt bad that I hadn't been home more.

When I told them how sorry I was that I kept missing so many of their ball games and other extracurricular activities they said, "It's okay, Mom. We know you need to be with Reed and Robert."

Mark and I felt so thankful that they never made us feel like they were being neglected even though, out of necessity, they were.

CHAPTER **13**

I WAS USUALLY very happy to help other people who were in need, but when it came to receiving help, it was an entirely different experience. After the accident, I'm sure I would have hesitated to accept all of the help people so kindly offered if I hadn't heard a story several years earlier that changed my way of thinking.

There was a man standing on his porch during a flood. As the water lapped upon his porch the man prayed, "Lord, save me!" Pretty soon someone in a canoe paddled by and said, "Hop aboard and I'll take you to higher ground." The man on the porch replied, "No thanks, the Lord will save me." After a while the man was standing on his roof as the water crept over it. Someone in a motorboat came by and said, "Hop on board and I'll take you to higher ground." The man on the roof said, "No thanks, the Lord will save me." A short time later the man was treading water when a helicopter flew over him dropping a rope. "Grab on to the line and I'll pull you up and take you to higher ground," called a voice. Still treading water, the man replied, "No thanks, the Lord will save me." A few minutes later the man drowned. When he went to heaven he asked the Lord why, when he had so much faith, didn't He save him? The Lord answered, "Well, what did you want? I sent you two boats and a helicopter!"

Friends, neighbors, and church members were anxious to do anything they could to help us get through our challenges each day, and we graciously accepted their help, knowing it was the Lord's way of blessing us. These wonderful people brought meals to our home almost every night for several months, and women took turns driving me the forty-five miles to the hospital every morning, so that when Mark joined me there after work, we could drive home together and talk about everything that had gone on during the day.

Even people we had never met wanted to help us. In the VA hospital, a 65-year-old man in a room down the hall from Reed had been a quadriplegic for forty years and was dying of cancer. He was not expected to live more than a few days. His daughters came to us and said that their father wanted our family to have his handicap-accessible van for Reed and Robert. We couldn't believe our ears! Here was a family who, in the midst of their sorrow, blessed our lives. We hadn't even considered how we would get our sons home, but a way was already provided.

We were blessed with another example of compassion and generosity when five builders in Northborough and the surrounding towns each felt impressed to contact each other about helping our family. They would build an 1,100 square foot addition onto our house so that we could bring Reed and Robert home when they were well enough. The Nixon Associates, as they called themselves, arranged a meeting with us to explain their plan. They would build the addition according to our specifications, and all we would have to do was pay for the building materials.

We had already been given a van, and now these amazing men who didn't know us at all wanted to build an addition onto our house for us! We didn't know what to say except, "Thank you, from the bottom of our hearts."

By the time that beautiful addition was finished, the Nixon Associates told us that part of the materials had been donated by other businesses and that they had decided to split the remaining cost five ways, so we wouldn't have to pay a penny. It was a gift beyond belief!

Reed's and Robert's teammates planned their fundraisers for the third week in June. A lot of planning was needed to pull off so many different events, so they held planning meetings each week for two months before the events took place. Mark tried to attend whenever he could, but one night when he couldn't get away from work, I went to the meeting. I was late because I had a dead battery at the hospital. When I finally got to the meeting, I was shocked to see about fifty teenagers and adults jam-packed into the room! I sat there, completely amazed, as each committee reported the progress they'd made and how much money was in the fund so far—$40,000—twice the total everyone was hoping for. And they were only halfway through!

At home Robert had always been called by his full name, but that night I heard everyone calling him Rob. I had not yet considered the fact that Robert was changing, not only physically, but on a deeper, more individual level as well. Robert had seemingly transformed before my eyes from a little boy to a man who was battling insurmountable odds and developing an identity outside of our family. The next day at the hospital I asked Robert if he wanted us to call him Rob. He said, "Sure," and he has been called Rob ever since.

The fundraisers began in June with a high school dance. Over two hundred students attended. The next day, four shops in the Northborough Shopping Plaza decided to give a portion of their sales that day to the Reed and Rob Nixon Trust Fund. Outside of the shops, high school students sold a hot dog and drink for a dollar and earned $300, while across the street there was a car wash that had a steady stream of cars all day long and brought in $1,000. Next in the string of fundraisers was a golf tournament that added $10,000 to the fund!

Mark and I were presented with an official certificate from Northborough City declaring June 17, 1995, Reed and Rob Nixon Day. It began with a 5K road race. The planners of the race were hoping for two hundred runners, but even before the day of the race five hundred people were pre-registered! It was a beautiful morning and there was excitement in the air, almost like a community carnival. We thought that by the time the race started we might have another two hundred runners, but when the gun went off 1,053 runners and walkers took off. The Reed and Rob Nixon race was later reported to be the fourth largest road race in Massachusetts that year.

First benefit race

After the race a woman told Mark that years before, her daughter had been seriously injured when she was fifteen, "... but when I went through this, I withdrew inside myself and didn't let people help me. I think this is so remarkable. People should appreciate the fact that your family has allowed them to help you. And look what it has done for so many." People often said to us, "Thank you for letting us help you."

As soon as the race was over and awards were handed out, Mark and Raelene went to the hospital to make sure everything was still on schedule for Reed and Rob to attend the banquet that night, the last of the fundraisers their teammates had organized for them. It would be the first time Reed and Rob had left the hospital, so the doctors and nurses were a little nervous about it, especially since usually when a patient left the hospital for the first time, they went home for about thirty minutes and then came straight back to the hospital. The banquet would be more like four hours plus two hours to get there and back, so the staff had good reason to be concerned.

CHAPTER **14**

CAMERA LIGHTS FLASHED and people cheered as Reed and Rob made their way into the banquet hall. Mark and I felt like they were celebrities rolling down the red carpet to attend the premier of a new movie. Everyone was so excited to see the boys and Reed and Rob, having never received so much attention in their whole lives, were especially happy and excited.

The banquet was sold out, with three hundred people in attendance. Reed wasn't able to eat any food there because he was still relearning to swallow and he was on a liquid diet, but Natalie kept feeding him ice cream (a liquid, right?) and Reed said it was "the best vanilla ice cream I've had in a long time!" After dinner, the program began with my singing a song I'd previously written. I wanted to express my love and appreciation to everyone there and the whole community.

Every now and then, or maybe once in a lifetime,
We might find someone unique, unlike the rest,
Who's Christ-like, one who loves and one who cares,
One who offers help we need....

Angel of Light, that's what you are.
You've given me so much love.
Throughout my life, you'll seem to be
An Angel of Light from above...

Now through my life I'll try to be
An Angel of Light from above.

From, Angel of Light, Sheryl Nixon, 1989

A gentle spirit filled the room and many people were crying. Then Mark spoke about a pebble tossed into a pond with
the ripples in the water moving outward until they reached
the banks. He compared this to how we were feeling. Our
cups were drained every day, but with the help and support
we received from all of them, we felt like we had a whole
reservoir to dip our empty cups into. Sometimes the reservoir
ran over and the spill gates opened, blessing and touching
the lives of many others in the process. Then Mark thanked
everyone for keeping our reservoir full so we could keep filling our empty cups.

Rob thanked everyone for their kindness, but he became
emotional and said, "I have to stop talking before I start crying." He gave the microphone back and then Reed spoke for
about ten minutes. He had everyone laughing one minute,
crying the next, and then laughing again. It was clear that
Reed loved being there. Both Reed and Rob's personalities
were bright and full of joy. Everyone there loved hearing them
speak and sharing some of their experiences.

When the banquet was over, the nurse told us it was time
to take the boys back to the hospital, but Reed and Rob didn't
want to leave. There was still going to be a raffle and a dance.
They had seen some of the donated items to be raffled, like a
Patriots jersey signed by Drew Bledsoe and tickets to a Boston
Bruins game, so they really wanted to stay. But we had an
hour's drive back to the hospital, so it was best to leave while
the boys were still having a good time. Reed told Mark, "I
don't want to go back to the hospital yet, Dad."

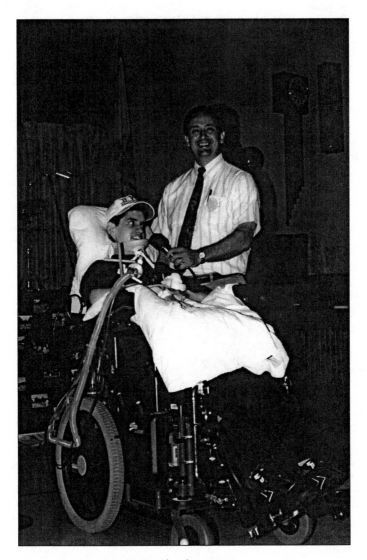

Reed at banquet

Rob at banquet

Mark had to say, "Reed, I'm sorry, but this is not my call. I'd let you stay if I could, but it's not up to me, so you have to go."

Just before we drove off, the chairman of the banquet pulled Mark aside and said, "When Reed was being loaded back in the van, he thanked me. That was all I needed to make this whole thing worthwhile."

It was a good thing we all left when we did, because by the time we got back to the hospital Reed and Rob were exhausted and anxious to get to bed. When Mark and I were ready to leave, Reed said, "Let's do it all again! Let's have another banquet next Saturday!"

On our way home from the hospital Mark said, "This was a very spiritual experience tonight. You know, tomorrow we're back in the real world, but we'll continue to receive strength. We'll be able to look back on this night and remember that we have a lot of people supporting us. We have met dozens of families who have shown that they want to help us and would be offended if we didn't ask them for help when we need it." After such a warm and wonderful evening, we wouldn't hesitate to ask them, either.

As Mark and I thought about the incredibly strong spirit we felt at the banquet, Mark suggested that maybe it was because everyone there had already opened their hearts and sacrificed to give us love and service, "and when that happens, God sends his spirit, so everyone involved in the fund-raisers, anyone who made donations, sent cards and letters, anyone who helped in any way, felt the sweetness of God's spirit touch their lives."

The total raised from the fundraisers came to $75,000! And that didn't include the gifts of the van and the addition to our house. Even with the incredible success of the fundraisers, more donations continued to pour in. One Sunday the priest of a nearby Catholic church announced that the next week there would be a second collection to be given to the Nixon brothers. The following Sunday people came with their checks already made out to the boys' trust fund. One parish member said she "saw people going for everything they had, digging deep in their pockets to come up with some cash." We were amazed again when the Catholic church gave us $4,200 from their congregation.

In the end, people said that they had never been so involved in a community effort, and that they had made more friends than they had in the past six, twelve, or even nineteen years living in Northborough. Still others said that being involved in helping Reed and Rob had been one of the best experiences they'd ever had—a highlight in their lives. Many lives were blessed even as they blessed ours.

CHAPTER **15**

THROUGHOUT THE REST of the summer, Mark and I were kept very busy learning how to help Reed and Rob progress. We had to know and be able to perform every single aspect of their care before they could come home in the fall.

Reed wanted to try breathing by himself, so with the help of the speech therapist, we unhooked the ventilator. He was on his own for a minute and a half, but none of us could tell if he was breathing on his own or not. Mark asked Reed what being off the ventilator felt like. Reed replied, "It feels like I haven't had a breath for a long time!" Mark and I thought Reed couldn't breathe at all without the ventilator—perhaps never would. He has remained vent-dependent.

Reed was constantly bogged down with infections and viruses. He got shingles from a dormant chicken pox virus that had remained in his system since childhood. Then he had surgery to remove some kidney stones that had shown up. Reed often had urinary tract infections (UTIs) because his bladder wouldn't drain properly. The urine pooled in his bladder and caused bacteria to build up until an infection began. He finally had surgery to cut the sphincter muscles in his bladder (muscles that hold the urine in the bladder) so his urine could run freely into a collection bag.

Mark and I gradually learned everything involved in Reed and Rob's care. The VA nurses showed us how to give them physical therapy (PT), so we could perform range of motion exercises on their hands, arms, and legs to keep their joints flexible. We started with their fingers, moving each joint back and forth five times before going to the next joint. In the future when science and medicine find a way to repair spinal cord injuries, flexible joints will be the key to regaining any physical movement.

Since Reed's chest muscles didn't work, he couldn't cough to get rid of mucus, so Mark and I had to suction his lungs. Because the procedure was a sterile one, we had to learn to put on sterilized gloves without contaminating them with our own skin's bacteria. Then we put a soft, narrow, sterilized catheter (about eighteen inches long) down Reed's trachea tube until it reached the top of his lungs. At first we were afraid of putting the catheter down too far and hurting Reed, but after several tries we realized that there was a point where we met resistance. At that point we didn't go any further and started the suction. Mark and I were each tested on the procedure until we could do it perfectly.

In August Reed got the new tongue touch keypad (TTK) retainer we ordered a couple of months before. It fit up in the roof of his mouth like a retainer someone might get after having braces taken off their teeth, but the TTK had a flat bottom with nine different buttons, each with a raised bump so Reed could distinguish one button from another. Reed had nine modes to control his environment. A chair mode with eight directions and four speeds let Reed drive his own wheelchair. He even had a cruise control where all he had to do was steer. The media mode allowed him to turn on and off the TV, stereo, VCR, DVD and cable. It also had a computer mode, and Reed's tongue controlled the mouse.

03/21/2011

TTK keypad

When Reed's tongue pushed a button on the TTK, a signal was sent to a receiver on the back of his headrest. The receiver sent the information to the control box on his wheelchair. The signals were sent by infrared or radio frequency. He had a small screen mounted next to his armrest so he could see what mode he was in.

Reed frequently got a kick out of asking people to guess how he drove his wheelchair. Since they couldn't see his TTK, they often guessed that his headrest had some special mechanism in it that drove his chair for him. Sometimes he teased people by telling them that he "just thought really hard and his chair moved." It was amazing how many people actually believed him. They were always fascinated when I took the TTK out of Reed's mouth and explained that Reed did everything with his tongue. The technology was truly amazing!

With the TTK as his environmental control unit, Reed was able to be independent with a few things.

Reed began working with voice-activated computer software called Dragon Dictate. After speaking about two hundred words into the computer microphone, he was able to speak loud enough for the computer to recognize and register his voice. Reed still uses voice-activated software with his computer.

Reed's cuff was gradually deflated more often, allowing him more time to speak. As time went on the cuff was deflated at night, as well. However, after a week with Reed's cuff deflated all the time, our hopes were shattered. I got a call from the hospital at 7:15 one morning telling me that Reed had gone into seizures and had been taken to the ICU. I blinked and struggled to maintain control of my emotions as I rushed to the hospital.

Shortly after I got to Reed's room, he started into another seizure. He thrashed around in the bed with involuntary muscle spasms, his tongue hanging out, and his eyes twitching and rolling back. I panicked as I hit the nurse's call button and yelled that something was wrong! I was immediately hustled out of Reed's room and left alone only to imagine the worst. Would Reed's delicate life end right then and there? Would I have to call Mark with the unthinkable? Would we now have to see Reed suffer with constant seizures, or something even worse, such as no brain function? Would I ever again see Reed alive?

I broke down and cried in the silence of the waiting room. With all the strength I could muster, I prayed for help from the Lord. It felt like an eternity before a nurse came out of Reed's room. I leaped up from my seat and rushed to her side! Reed was alive! Thank the Lord! However, I wasn't allowed in the room until the doctors and nurses had him stabilized. I was still totally and unmercifully left unaware of the details of his condition. Finally I was told that since Reed's cuff had been deflated longer each day, even at night, too much carbon dioxide was in his blood, which had caused his electrolytes to be out of balance and his body to go into seizures. From that time on he would always need his cuff inflated while sleeping at night.

I spoke on the phone with Mark several times during the day for support and comfort. Eventually he arrived at the hospital that evening after work. Reed was sedated and asleep when Mark came to his bedside. He touched Reed's hand and was surprised that it was ice-cold! The nurses had assumed that because I was with Reed, they didn't need to check him as often. They figured I would come and get them if anything was wrong. However, because I had allowed myself to slip emotionally, and I hadn't maintained my composure throughout the day, I wasn't able to pay close enough attention to what was going on. I felt embarrassed and ashamed, as if for some reason it was my responsibility. Losing control of my emotions meant that I had inadvertently lost my ability to focus on Reed's needs. Mark was surprised at the hospital's lack of awareness and quickly grabbed a thermometer to take Reed's temperature. It was 92 degrees! He hit the nurse's call button and shouted for help! Instantly the room filled with doctors and nurses trying everything to get Reed's body warmed up! I wondered, "With Reed in the ICU *how is it* that his vital signs got missed?" I realized that I couldn't always rely on the medical staff for every detail. I knew that I absolutely *could not* allow myself to lose control again! Looking back now, I realize that I never did tell Mark about my feelings of letting Reed down.

The next several days I stayed with Reed at the hospital day and night, singing to him, reading to him, and wiping away his tears. During those days in the ICU I had a hard time communicating with Reed. He was extremely groggy, and his tongue was so swollen from continually biting it during the seizures that I had a difficult time reading his lips. Several days later Reed was completely stabilized and back in his room, but now when he looks to his far left or right, his eyes twitch.

ﮞﮞﮞ

In the meantime, Rob was making progress in his school work and physical therapy (PT). He had ten weeks of material to make up in order to finish his sophomore year in high school, and he was determined not to get further behind. With the help of several tutors at the hospital, Rob spent most of the summer trying to catch up. His goal was to finish high school on time and graduate with his class.

Rob was also working toward independence with his physical skills. At one point Mark and I had to decide whether Rob should have a power chair or a manual one. Rob medically qualified for a power chair, but we knew that if he started out in one it would be unlikely he would ever try a manual wheelchair. Our insurance company would pay for the first wheelchair, but if we got a manual one to start out with and it didn't work for Rob, we might have to buy the second chair ourselves, and they started at $25,000! Our family motto of maximization helped us make our decision. Rob needed to maximize any amount of movement that he had and push himself to achieve it.

Each day Rob had PT sessions that varied from learning how to brush his hair and teeth to learning how to drive. At the time of the accident Rob had had his learner's permit for about four weeks. Mark and I were very surprised when the doctors told us that they fully expected Rob to be able to drive by himself. We didn't know how that could possibly happen, so we met with a driving therapist to try to learn how we could help Rob step by step.

The therapist explained to us that modifications, such as a lowered floor, a raised ceiling, and a van lift or ramp, needed to be made to whatever van Rob would drive. A toggle switch on the driver's seat would allow Rob to rotate the seat to the right and back again, as well as move forward and back like a normal seat. That way, when he became strong enough, Rob could transfer himself from his wheelchair to the driver's seat and then turn the chair back toward the front to drive.

I'll never forget the first time Rob got behind the steering wheel of a van. It was definitely a lesson in patience. With the use of a slide board, two feet long by one foot wide, it took Rob an hour to gradually scoot himself from his wheelchair into the driver's seat. (See picture on page 184) I wanted to just boost him there. However, I couldn't be with him every time he drove, so I had to know if Rob would be able to transfer by himself. It took all I had to just stand there and watch him struggle. When he was finally in the seat, we helped him wrap his fingers around the key. But when he tried to start the van we were all terribly disappointed that he didn't have the strength in his wrist to turn the key. Tired and frustrated, we decided that was enough for one afternoon. We'd have to try again tomorrow.

Mark and I couldn't imagine how Rob would ever be able to drive by himself, but since the doctors had assured us that he would, we hung on to the hope that someday he would drive. We knew it was important to be patient and not let Rob see us discouraged. He needed our support and encouragement to be able to maximize his potential, even though Mark and I had no idea what his potential actually was. It turned out that within two years Rob was driving his own van: maximization worked.

Rob driving

Never give up the fight for right. Never give up at all.
Never give up the will to win, to stand up when you fall.
Never give up your heritage. You came from royal birth.
And always remember why you came to Earth....

We are here to prove ourselves, will we live righteously?
The choices we make in our lives decide our destiny.
Endure throughout the good and bad, that's what we're
asked to do.

And if we prove we're faithful, we'll be among those who will

Never give up the fight for right....
From, Never Give Up, Sheryl Nixon, 1986

Although Rob was progressing in school and therapy, he really struggled as he dealt with the constant pain. One source of his pain was spasms: sudden involuntary contractions of one or more of his muscles. Rob's spasms usually started in his feet and legs, and then traveled up through his whole body until everything shook. The shaking caused terrible pain in his neck. We were very careful when we touched him, because many times a touch was all it took to set off a series of spasms. Sometimes they were so strong that they almost knocked him out of bed. His foot got stuck in the railing of the bed during one particular spasm and he couldn't get it out. Mark spent several minutes fighting against the spasm to get Rob's leg to bend so he could get it unstuck. Mark finally worked it loose; he and Rob were both exhausted.

Another source of Rob's pain was having too much calcium in his blood. His bones were no longer weight-bearing, so the calcium sloughed off into his bloodstream, producing nausea. The doctors and nurses wanted Rob to drink three liters of water a day to flush the calcium out of his kidneys faster. The increase in fluids would also help him get some relief from the constipation he struggled with. The nurses brought prune juice for Rob to drink to loosen his bowels. When Rob complained to his dad about how awful the juice tasted, Mark said, "Look Rob, let me taste this stuff," being almost certain that Rob was just being picky. The nurse brought Mark a small glass of the juice and he drank it. He almost gagged! It wasn't ordinary prune juice; it was thick, concentrated prune juice with the consistency of syrup! Realizing Rob was not exaggerating, Mark said, "Rob, do you know what you need? You need your teeth brushed!"

CHAPTER 16

ON MONDAY, SEPTEMBER 25, 1995, I brought Rob home from the VA Hospital. The doctors thought it would be best to send one boy home at a time so Mark and I could learn one routine before adding another. Sending both boys home at the same time would just be too overwhelming. One of the nurses asked Mark if we were going to try to get each boy up every morning for their bowel routines and showers, and Mark told her that we were. She told Mark that she and several other nurses had been trying to imagine how we would do it. She said that even there at the hospital they did everything while the boys were in bed. Concerned, she said, "We don't know how you are going to be able to do it. How will you cope with everything? One paralyzed patient is hard enough, but two?" Mark told her we would just take it one day at a time.

> When I was just a little girl, I fell and hurt my knee.
> And I was just about as sad as a little girl could be.
> I had to use a wheelchair, then crutches every day,
> And when I'd get discouraged, I'd hear my mama say,
>
> You just take it...one day at a time.
> From, One Day at a Time, Sheryl Nixon, 1998

Reed was very excited for Rob to be able to come home, but he had a difficult time saying goodbye, and he couldn't hold back his tears. Reed knew he was scheduled to come home the following Monday, but he was afraid that he might have to stay longer if anything went wrong. He knew plans often changed suddenly for him.

Many of Rob's friends were at our house when he and I drove up. Rob was thrilled to see them. I pushed him up our new ramp and through the door of our new addition, but unfortunately, it wasn't quite finished. The linoleum wasn't down and there wasn't a stitch of furniture, not even a hospital bed to put Rob in. I told him everything was supposed to have been finished, but our building scheduler had just gotten a little behind. A couple of Rob's friends went upstairs to his old room, took apart his bed, brought it downstairs, and put it back together in his new room. I was pretty concerned about how I would take care of him without any equipment or supplies. I called Mark at work to ask him to stop by the hospital on his way home and find out what in the world we were supposed to do.

When Mark got home, he told me the hospital had called the supply company and, indeed, the equipment and supplies had not been sent. Over and over we discovered that the medical industry was not very customer-oriented. They presented themselves well in order to be competitive and get our business, but once they had the contract, their services weren't very reliable. Mark and I were happy to have Rob home, but we felt disorganized and unprepared. We were certainly glad the hospital hadn't sent Reed home first, because *his* care was much more involved and complicated than Rob's.

Our first night with Rob home was rough. Since I worked all day helping Rob, Mark said he would do the night turns. Rob needed to be turned onto his opposite side every few hours to avoid bed sores. I had purchased a baby monitor to put up in our bedroom so we could hear Rob call out to us if he needed anything during the night. At midnight Mark got Rob turned on his side and then went to bed himself. At 1:30 Rob woke up feeling a burning sensation and called out for his dad. Rob's leg had fallen over the side of the bed, which had caused the pain. Mark got Rob settled and went back to bed. About forty-five minutes later, just after Mark had fallen back to sleep, Rob called out again. He asked his dad what the strange noise was that he heard. Mark looked around and noticed that the heat vents were on, sending air up which was stirring a bouquet of welcome home balloons around creating the noise. Mark and Rob both laughed. Rob was afraid someone was outside vandalizing the house. "Sorry to bother you, Dad," he said.

Mark got up again at 6:00 to turn Rob on his other side, and again at 7:15 when the nurse arrived to help get Rob up and ready for the day. For the next hour or so, Mark trained the nurse in what to do. Several therapists arrived to evaluate Rob. Construction workers came to continue working on the addition, as well. The house was full of commotion all day long.

The next night as Mark turned Rob, Rob's catheter came off, and since he couldn't control his bladder, the bed got wet. Mark didn't know where the supplies had been put, nor had he ever put a condom catheter on either Reed or Rob. He finally got Rob all cleaned up, but the bed linens still needed changing. When he couldn't figure out how to change the sheets with Rob still in the bed, he woke me up. It took both of us forty-five minutes to get everything finished. As Mark and I left the room exhausted, Rob called out, "Not too bad for the first time, Dad."

Mark's heart melted and he said, "Thank you, Rob. I needed that."

The next Monday, October 2, Reed came home. I was annoyed and frustrated because the linoleum still wasn't finished and the supplies we received for Reed weren't the high quality of those we used at the hospital.

When we drove into our driveway, Reed was surprised and thrilled to see thirty of his cross-country teammates and friends with signs and banners there to welcome him home. But their visit ended when they had to leave an hour later to go to a cross-country meet at the high school. When Reed found out he said, "I want to go!"

Rob said, "Me too!"

I loaded them both into the van with Natalie and Kent, and we took off to see the races. At the end of the previous cross-country season, Reed had been selected as one of the captains of the team. Even though he couldn't participate, he wanted to be there to support his teammates. After the team won their meet, I took a picture of Reed and Rob with them. We hurried home to throw together an open house at our place for the team and some of the boys' other friends.

1995 Algonquin Regional High School cross-country team

But when everyone had gone home and we got the boys to bed, it took a long time for Reed to fall asleep. Nights were more difficult for him than days. When he couldn't fall asleep, he'd just lie awake thinking, and it was never good to have too much time to think in this situation. It was a sure-fire way to get depressed. Because I had chronic depression, I always watched for signs in any of my family after the accident so I could help them, but to my knowledge none of them except Natalie had a problem with depression.

Reed was more anxious at night, especially since the pop-off at the hospital when he passed out from lack of oxygen. He was afraid that something would go wrong while he was alone. He knew we were listening on the monitor, but he didn't know how long it would take to wake us up. He had to miss two breaths before his alarm sounded, and he didn't know how much more time would pass without oxygen before one of us got downstairs to his bedside. What if the power went out, shutting off the monitor? What if the ventilator malfunctioned and the alarm didn't go off? Or maybe Mark would sleep through the alarm and he would *never* wake up? Reed knew that too many things could go wrong.

Reed's first night at home was pretty scary because his cuff was inflated, so he couldn't call out if he needed anything. Even though Mark and I had the monitor, Reed could only click his tongue to get our attention, and Mark was afraid he wouldn't be able to hear the click and wake up. After getting Reed settled for the night, Mark set his alarm for 3 a.m. to wake up and turn Reed and Rob, and then he went to bed. At 1:30 Reed clicked his tongue, signaling that he needed something. Mark jumped out of bed, ran down the stairs, and asked how long Reed had been clicking. Reed said he had clicked only the one time and that he needed to be suctioned. Mark suctioned Reed's lungs and went back to bed, relieved that he had heard the click. From then on Mark slept more comfortably knowing that he would be able to wake up whenever Reed clicked. Between us, Mark is always the one who listens for Reed at night. I'm so grateful, since I need to wear earplugs to be able to sleep soundly.

CHAPTER **17**

REED'S FIRST NURSE at home was a pretty young woman, only twenty-three years old. After seeing Reed's nurse, Rob pulled his dad aside and said, "Dad, this is a rip!" Not knowing what Rob was referring to, Mark was concerned. Then Rob said, "Have you seen the pretty young nurse that Reed got? And I got a grandma for mine!" Mark was relieved, and they both had a good laugh.

One morning shortly after getting both boys home, Mark and I met with the VA Hospital's case workers, our insurance company's case manager, and the Visiting Nurses Association of Massachusetts, all of whom came to our house, to figure out what help we needed, how many hours of nursing our sons qualified for, and how to make the arrangements to get the help we needed. The case manager for our insurance company, along with a therapist, evaluated Reed and told Mark and me that Reed qualified for eighty-four hours of nursing a week. Rob qualified for thirty-two hours a week.

It was decided that Reed would get about twelve hours of nursing help each day for the first month, ten hours a day for the second month, and eight hours a day for the third month. Rob was given four hours a day for three months. After that, we would get our nursing and personal care attendant (PCA) hours through a Massachusetts state program called The Center for Living and Working (CLW). We would find and hire people to be the PCAs, and CLW would pay them. Mark and I would be responsible for Reed and Rob's care when nurses weren't there, basically the evening and night hours. We were told that we would train the nurses in Reed and Rob's care. The VA nurses had trained us very well, so we felt confident that we would be able to teach the nurses who came to our house what they needed to know to take care of our sons.

But our first month with nursing care for Reed and Rob was really awful. We discovered that most of the nurses didn't have training in trachea care or ventilators. Mark and I knew more than they did. It was a pretty uncomfortable situation. The worst part was that we had a different nurse almost every day, so training them didn't really do any good.

One particular morning, after three hours of teaching the nurse Reed's bowel and shower routine, Mark said, "It's a good thing I only have to train you once for when you come again."

The nurse said, "Well, I'm not coming back. This was just a one-time assignment. In fact, you know, you are really doing all of the work. I don't even know why I'm here."

Annoyed, Mark responded, "You're right, I don't know why you're here, either."

Mark knew it wasn't her fault, but he felt that the nursing agency really did us a disservice when they sent us someone for only one shift. Reed's care was very complicated, and a nurse couldn't just walk in and know what to do. By the end of the first month Mark and I felt like we had trained half of the nurses in Massachusetts!

Reed and Rob were really happy to be home, but having nurses who didn't know what to do for them made them very nervous, especially Reed. One evening Mark and I had a 7:00 church meeting to go to, and Mark was one of the speakers. The nurse was supposed to be at our house promptly at 6:00 p.m. so we could leave, but she didn't arrive until 6:15. We didn't have much time to train her in Reed's routine. We were just ready to walk out the door when the nurse came and told us that Reed wanted to see us. When we walked into Reed's room, his eyes looked as big as saucers! He was practically beside himself and the look on his face said, "Don't you dare leave me alone with this lady!"

Reed told us that the nurse had just tried to go down his trachea tube with the yankauer (a hard plastic device to suction saliva from his mouth) instead of the soft, sterile plastic catheter that she was supposed to use to go down into his lungs and suction up mucus.

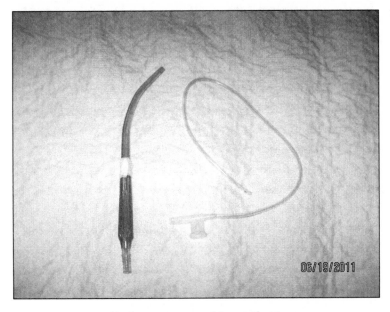

Yankauer versus suction catheter

The nurse had told us that she'd had twenty years of experience and knew how to do suctioning and trachea care. We didn't know what experience she actually had, but because she had told us that she knew how to do suctioning, we didn't train her on it. When we realized that she wasn't as experienced as she had said, Mark and I suctioned Reed's lungs. Then, knowing that his dad had to speak at the meeting, Reed said, "Dad leave. You are going to be late anyway. Just leave." So we did.

Mark began his talk with, "We thought that with the kids grown up we wouldn't have to worry about babysitters anymore."

Then he explained why he was late.

Mark and I got home and the nurse left. Reed told us that while we were gone she spilled his pills all over the floor and broke his thermometer. Because he didn't trust her, he hadn't let her feed him or do anything for him while we were gone. He was so upset that he cried as he told us what had happened. It broke our hearts that Reed had felt mistreated. I'm sure the nurse was trying her best to help Reed, but because we expected a trained nurse and got an untrained nurse, our expectations weren't realized.

Mark told Reed that it was okay to feel bad, but not to dwell on it. He said that Reed needed to pray and ask for strength, and that we would do all we could to make things better for him. Mark and I realized that not only did *we* need to know everything about Reed's care, *Reed* needed to know everything about his care so he could make sure he was taken care of correctly. Now if he sees anything not quite right, he corrects the nurses and PCAs himself.

Mark and I were awakened early one morning the following week with a knock at our bedroom door. Someone said that Reed wanted us right away. When Mark and I got downstairs to Reed's bedroom, we were shocked to see the same nurse that had given us so much trouble the week before. Reed asked the nurse to leave the room while he talked to us.

He explained to us that his bowel and shower routine was supposed to be that morning, but that the nurse had no idea what to do. She had suctioned his lungs and then forgotten to put his ventilator back on to give him some breaths before going down to suction him again. And then when she had turned him on his side, his head had started rolling off the pillow. Reed had yelled, "Watch out for my head!" In trying to stop Reed's head, she somehow moved his neck the wrong way. He heard and felt a pop in his neck and it really hurt him. Reed was furious! "Why is she treating me this way? And why doesn't she know what to do?"

Reed was fed up and wanted the nurse to leave. Mark went out of the room and kindly asked her to go. She felt bad that Reed was upset. Mark told her not to worry about it and that we would take care of him for the rest of the day.

Mark came back into Reed's room and said, "Reed, you have got to know that we are going to back you up on your care. You have never been a complainer and you haven't changed in the past six months, so we believe you. We want you to know that we will always stick by you and that you can count on us to look after you." After that we wondered if we would ever feel comfortable leaving Reed at home.

As time went on, sometimes I had to leave the boys with a nurse or PCA while I ran my errands, but I still worried about them. Every time I heard a siren or saw an ambulance my stomach churned, afraid it was rushing to *my* house because something was wrong with Reed or Rob. They were so fragile, and either of them could take a turn for the worse in a matter of minutes. Without a cell phone, I had no way of knowing what was happening at home.

Now when I hear a siren or see an ambulance I don't worry as much because I always have a cell phone with me so I can be reached. However, my heart always goes out to that family whose lives may have just been changed forever. Then I offer a silent prayer in their behalf. I'm very grateful I'm many years down the road of our new life instead of back during those first months and years of uncertainty and constant change.

◆◆◆◆

Mark and I chose early on to alternate Reed and Rob's bowel and shower days, since it took all morning just to get one son finished. Mark came downstairs one morning and saw that Rob's nurse had gotten him dressed and in his wheelchair, but when Mark told the nurse that it was supposed to be Rob's shower and bowel care day, the nurse said, "What is bowel care?" Mark couldn't believe his ears. The nurse had another client and had to leave. Mark took care of Rob's morning routine and trained another new nurse for Reed at the same time, so I could stay asleep. Even though I continually tried to be alert and on top of everything that needed to be done, I was so exhausted day in and day out that Mark did all he could to let me sleep as long as possible. He was probably hoping to avoid my having a physical and emotional meltdown.

When Reed and Rob came home after six months in the hospital, Mark and I were expecting to have nursing "help." We ended up with nurses who had general nursing background, but had little or no experience with ventilators, trachea care, or even quadriplegics. I suppose it was a case of expectation versus realization; we expected the nurses to be like the VA nurses had been, but that wasn't our reality. At the time, however, we hadn't realized that Reed's care was so specialized and complicated. We had to teach every single nurse who came to our home how to take care of him. It was a tremendous amount of work.

We didn't just have trouble with the nurses at home. Occasionally when Reed was in the hospital overnight we struggled with the nurses there, too. I stayed with Reed most of the days and evenings when he had to be in the hospital, and many times I slept there. One night I explained to the nurse that since Reed couldn't push a call button to get her attention during the night, he would click his tongue, so she needed to listen carefully for the click. I told her that I would be sleeping in the waiting room and to come and get me if Reed needed me.

At 3:00 a.m. the nurse woke me up and said that Reed wanted me. Reed told me that he had asked the nurse to turn him on his side, but she had just put a pillow behind his shoulder, so his back and bottom were still touching the bed. He said he ached all over. He also told me he had been clicking for an hour trying to get the nurse's attention because he was so uncomfortable, but he had finally given up. When she came in at the regularly scheduled time during the night, Reed asked, "Why didn't you come when I clicked?" Didn't you hear me clicking?"

She told him she thought it was the rain, but Reed said she wasn't very convincing and he didn't believe her. He thought she was just doing other things and wasn't really listening for him well enough. I felt that even if the nurse had thought it was the rain she should have gone to check on Reed to make sure everything was all right. I turned Reed on his side like he was used to being turned at home, had the nurse get him some morphine for his pain, and went back to sleep after he was settled.

The next day I wondered how Reed could feel pain when he was paralyzed. I learned that even though Reed's central nervous system didn't work, each of our bodies has a secondary mechanism for sensation called the sympathetic nervous system. This system uses nerves that don't go through the spinal cord. It helps control blood pressure, digestion, heart rate, bowels, and the bladder. Most pain signals use nerves that go through the central nervous system, but in Reed the signals don't reach his brain because of his injury. However, the sympathetic nervous system sometimes responds to the pain through phantom pain, as well as referred pain. While an able-bodied person would feel uncomfortable in minutes, it could take hours for Reed to recognize the discomfort. Sometimes he would hurt everywhere. Other times he'd describe a specific pain such as, "my knee hurts," when in fact his toe was bent back in his shoe, causing the pain. He was unable to determine exactly where the pain came from like a healthy person would. But he still *felt* the pain.

One day Reed got very sick, so we took him to the hospital. He was admitted and ended up having to stay eight days. I stayed with him as much as I could, but I still had Rob, Natalie, and Kent to take care of at home. Most of those days, by the time I got the other kids off to school and myself to the hospital, Reed was miserable. Because he had trouble swallowing, there were days that I arrived and found his mouth completely full of saliva! Before doing anything else, I grabbed a cup for him to spit into.

The nurses were just too busy to keep a close eye on him. Many times I arrived to find Reed in a lot of pain because the nurses hadn't turned him often enough or far enough on his side to give his back and bottom a rest. Still other times Reed's condom catheter had come off. By the time I got to the hospital he had been lying in a urine-soaked bed for a long time. In the whole eight days Reed was in the hospital, he was given only one bath. He came home with a bad rash all over his groin. Mark and I quickly learned that the hospital was not a particularly good place to be when you're sick. We knew our sons got much better care at home, so we avoided the hospital whenever we could.

As time has passed we now have a wonderful, stable group of knowledgeable nurses who have loved and cared for Reed for many years. It's made all the difference in Reed's care, as well as significantly lightening Mark's and my load. We no longer have to worry every time we leave Reed home alone with a nurse. Besides, we always have our cell phones with us and can be reached immediately if anything goes wrong.

We also have a group of wonderful doctors who actually know Reed inside and out. They all work together to help him enjoy the best quality of life possible. We are able to take care of most of the issues at home, but when necessary, we know what to do at the hospital. Having been to the same hospital for sixteen years now, they know us well and we trust them more.

CHAPTER 18

I MENTIONED EARLIER that Reed and Rob loved to tease their sisters, but their teasing didn't stop there; they loved to give their therapists and nurses a hard time, too. The humor added some much-needed cheerfulness to a pretty dismal situation.

It started in the VA hospital when Rob was in one of his therapy sessions. The therapist was teaching Rob how to handle some of his personal care, like combing his hair. Since Rob's hands didn't work, the therapist had taken Rob's comb and attached a plastic loop on the top so that Rob's hand could slip inside the loop to hold the comb instead of holding it with his fingers. Then Rob's arm would move his hand and comb to fix his hair. When the therapist attached the loop, a couple of the teeth on the comb melted a bit and were kind of deformed. She told Rob she was sorry and hoped it was all right. Rob told her that the comb was a gift his aunt had brought him from Paris and its cost and sentimental value made it priceless. The therapist was distraught and apologized over and over. Rob finally had to admit to her that he had just been kidding.

Later that day when the therapist had a session with Reed, she told Reed that Rob had played a dirty trick on her and she explained it to him. Reed and Rob hadn't seen each other yet that day, but Reed picked right up on the joke and told the therapist that Rob's comb really was a gift from his aunt. Reed said, "Rob just told you he was kidding because he didn't want you to feel bad." The therapist almost started crying, believing that Rob had been more worried about her feelings than his own. A little later the therapist found out that both Reed and Rob had been teasing her. She wasn't quite as quick to fall for their jokes after that.

One day, with a straight face, Reed told his nurse that he thought he was getting gangrene on his wrist from the medical ID bracelet he had worn for almost five months. Even though the nurse knew better, Reed was so convincing that she looked under the bracelet and then back at Reed. When she saw a huge smile on his face she knew he had tricked her again.

At home Reed and Rob continued teasing their nurses. Both boys had to wear special booties at night to keep their feet in the correct position. Each booty could fit on either foot. When a nurse started to put the booties on, the boys said, "No, wait a minute. That booty goes on the other foot." The nurse stopped and traded feet. "Wait, I was wrong. It goes on the other foot." Not recognizing the joke the nurse stopped again and traded booties. The poor woman might have been trading booties all evening if the boys hadn't cracked up laughing.

As time went on we recognized that the boys teased only when they were feeling well and were in good moods. It got so we really missed the teasing when one or both of them were sick for days at a time. When the teasing started up again we knew they were feeling better. We were all glad for it, even though none of us liked to be the one that got tricked. Reed and Rob were never mean; they just liked a good joke.

When unexpected things happened we tried to learn to laugh at them, too. Rob had a doctor's appointment at UMASS one day, so I got him loaded up in the van and we took off— late as usual. When I turned left from our cul-de-sac onto the main road, I accelerated too quickly. I heard a loud clump!

When I looked back, I saw Rob and his wheelchair tipped completely over! How could I be so careless? I was trying so hard to help my sons and here I was causing more pain! Was it really that important to be on time to a doctor's appointment? I decided I needed to get my priorities straight.

I put my hazard warning lights on and climbed into the back to help Rob up. I was expecting to see him hurt and angry, but he was laughing! I certainly couldn't laugh. All I could do was tell Rob how sorry I was over and over. That just made him laugh harder! I'm continually amazed at Rob's great sense of humor and his desire to make others comfortable when they are around him, despite his own discomfort.

Rob was too heavy and the wheelchair was too awkward for me to get him sitting back up. I didn't know what else to do, so I got out of the van and waved down the next car that came by and asked the driver to help me. The man was very kind and soon Rob was back up in his wheelchair. However, his condom catheter had come off, so he was wet. We hurried back home and called the doctor's office to let them know we would be even later. I got Rob cleaned up, dressed, and back in his chair and we were on our way again. All the way to the doctor's office I continued to apologize, but Rob just laughed and told me not to worry about it. That night when I told everybody what had happened, they all laughed, but I cried.

꙳꙳꙳

Rob started back to school at Algonquin on November 1. In the beginning he wasn't very excited about going back to school because he was afraid he would be too far behind. But he had way too much free time at home with nothing to do; he *needed* to be back in school. Reed wasn't able to go back to school because his morning routine took so long that by the time he was dressed, in his wheelchair, and to school, it was nearly time for school to be out.

Rob's first day back to school started off pretty hectic. A wheelchair-accessible school bus was going to pick him up at 9:30, so Mark and I had him up, dressed, and ready to go. At 9:25 we realized Rob's condom catheter had become disconnected from his leg bag, so he was wet. His biggest fear in going to school was that he would end up wet and have to come home.

Mark and I quickly got him back into bed, cleaned him up, changed his clothes, and got him back in his chair. The whole time Rob was saying, "Hurry! Hurry!"

Finally Mark said, "Relax, Rob. There's no way you can miss this bus. The bus driver isn't going to leave without you, because you're the only one on the bus. You can't be late." Rob relaxed a little after that, but he was still pretty anxious about his first day back to school. Mark continued, "Rob, the worst thing that could happen at school has already happened, so just relax and you'll have a really good day."

At the end of the school day Rob came home smiling and announced that at least he hadn't run anyone down in the halls. He was happy to be back in school, and all of his friends were glad to see him again, too.

Rob was tutored in Spanish at home, but he kept up on everything else at school. Not only did Rob like being with his friends, but he enjoyed participating in a lot of the school activities, as well. For example, two girlfriends invited him to go with them to a play at the high school, so Mark helped get Rob in their car, folded down his wheelchair, and the three friends took off. After the play the girls asked a football player to lift Rob back into their car and they drove him home.

Rob went to a lot of school dances, too. He rolled around the floor for the fast dances, and during the slow ones he had the girl sit with him on his lap in the wheelchair and they rolled around to the music. During high school Rob actually had a steady girlfriend two different times. He was very good-looking and had a great personality. Rob's ego was boosted when he realized that girls were still attracted to him even though he was in a wheelchair. That year he took his girlfriend to the Junior Prom.

CHAPTER 19

WITHIN THE FIRST year after the accident, Rob made quite a bit of physical improvement. One evening when Mark came home from work Natalie yelled to him, "Dad! Rob can move his finger!"

Mark looked at Rob and said, "What?"

Rob replied, "Yeah, look at this." Rob moved his middle finger. Since Rob teased us so much, Mark looked very closely to see if Rob was moving his wrist or arm to make the finger move. He even isolated Rob's wrist to prove it was just his finger moving. He *did* have some movement back in his fingers!

Rob exclaimed, "Dad, it's still coming back!"

When Mark helped Rob get ready for bed that night, Rob said, "I'd give it up."

Mark said, "What did you say?"

Rob repeated, "I'd give it up."

Mark said, "What do you mean?"

Rob looked right at Mark and said, "Dad, I'd give up all of the finger motions if Reed could just get anything back. I'd give up anything I've got if it would help him."

This wasn't an insincere wish. Rob had consistently demonstrated his willingness to sacrifice for Reed.

Mark thought about what Rob had said and explained, "Well Rob, it's nice that your successes don't come at the cost of Reed. We can all be happy for your successes; it's not a competition. However, because we are happy for you doesn't take anything away from Reed."

Rob went on to make progress, and two months later he wiggled his toes on both feet.

But Reed didn't seem to progress at all. Mark and I felt like he was taking one step forward in his progression and then five steps back.

It seemed Reed always struggled with one problem on top of another. It was common medical practice for a trachea tube (the tube that went directly into Reed's neck) to be changed quite often in order to avoid scar tissue building up at the site. At first Reed was scheduled to have his trachea tube changed once a month, but his scar tissue built up so fast that his trachea changes were too traumatic. As a result, the doctor decided to surgically make Reed's trachea opening larger.

Instead of just a slit, the doctor cut a small square-shaped opening. Reed was in the hospital for eight days. The nurses in the ICU were so busy that Reed frequently didn't get the care he needed, so I stayed with him most of the days and slept at the hospital every night. Since Reed had a different nurse every shift, I tried to show them how he liked to be taken care of. However, most of the nurses had their own way of doing things. Some of the nurses were happy for my suggestions, but others treated me like I didn't know a thing. How dare I tell them, the professionals, how to do something!

When Reed got home from the hospital, Mark and I realized there was a problem with his trachea site. The doctor had put a square opening in, but the tube itself was round. Maybe he thought the square would close in as it healed around the tube, but that wasn't happening, at least not fast enough. Reed had such a bad air leak around the tube that he could barely speak. Even the quality of his voice sounded worse.

The whole week after coming home, Reed didn't feel good and seldom got out of bed. He said he didn't feel like eating anything, but then in the next breath he'd complain about not having any energy. Mark and I had a terrible time getting him to eat or drink anything, and his weight was dropping fast. Before the accident Reed weighed around 130 pounds, but now he weighed only about 95 pounds and he looked more like a concentration camp prisoner than an athlete.

When Reed was in the hospital he didn't like the taste of the food, and sometimes even my home cooking didn't taste right to him. He told me that chocolate and orange juice didn't taste like they had before the accident. With the ventilator breathing for him, the air never went up into his nose so he had a hard time smelling. Smelling is such a huge part of tasting that it was no wonder his taste changed. As a result, Reed no longer enjoyed or looked forward to eating: it had become a chore.

Although I mentioned a little about Reed's swallowing issues in Chapter 9, there were some other reasons he had a difficult time eating. For instance, after chewing so long and swallowing so many times just to get one bite down, Reed felt like he'd already eaten a whole meal when he'd had only a little bit. Then, because it took Reed such a long time to get a couple of bites down, his food always got cold and had to be reheated. After several times in the microwave oven the food got pretty yucky.

Reed also had to learn the timing between swallowing and breathing so that he wouldn't accidentally swallow food into his lungs and get pneumonia. Another thing that made Reed not want to eat was that he began having a lot of pain in his chest, especially after he ate. We had multiple tests run trying to find out what the problem was, but there was never a diagnosis.

At home Mark and I tried to encourage Reed to eat and

drink more, but his trachea site leaked air so much that he usually felt too dizzy and sick to eat. We even tried scolding him, but that only made us all upset. We didn't know what to do and Reed was getting thinner and thinner. His calorie intake was so low that we knew if we didn't do something soon, he would either end up in the hospital with IVs and feeding tubes or starve to death.

Reed's not eating and drinking was also contributing to his body's not healing properly after the trachea surgery. His skin was supposed to close around the trachea tube so that the leak would stop, but without proper nourishment and hydration, it wouldn't close. Mark and I tried to get Reed to drink six to eight glasses of water each day for a whole week so he wouldn't have to get an IV, but we were unsuccessful. After all, it wasn't like we were dealing with a child. We couldn't force it down him.

Finally one night, Mark and Reed got into an argument about Reed's not eating and drinking. Reed didn't feel like eating because he felt sick, but he felt sick because he wasn't eating! If he would just eat and drink a little bit during the day, we wouldn't have the hassle every night. As it was, we were trying to get a whole day's worth of food and liquids down him at night in a two-hour period, and it wasn't working.

Only a week after Reed's first trachea surgery, he had to go back to the hospital to have his trachea tube changed a second time. Mark and I expressed our concern, but Reed's doctor still thought the skin would close in around the tube and wanted us to give it more time. We did everything we could think of to get the air into Reed's lungs instead of its leaking out of the hole in his neck. We had been laying the dressing over the hole, but Mark had recently seen the doctor tap the dressing down in and around the hole, so we tried that. Even though we tried to be careful, dressing the trachea tube was traumatic because Reed was still in a lot of pain from the surgery. The tube had just been changed two weeks before, so the tissue was still very tender.

When Reed first came home after this second surgery, he had a hard time swallowing because the anesthesia had stopped his swallowing reflex. That meant that he hadn't had his noon or evening medications and he hadn't had anything to eat or drink all day. Mark told Reed that he couldn't go to sleep until he had eaten something and had something to drink. Mark kept after him until Reed said, "Why are you doing this to me?"

Mark answered, "Because I have to. You are not going to sleep tonight until you eat a meal and drink some water." Reed finally finished the meal and drink at 1:00 in the morning, and he was already feeling better. He even felt better the next morning and ate some breakfast.

But each day we had to start all over again trying to push eating and drinking. We were up late night after night trying to convince Reed to eat and drink. Mark was so frustrated that he finally said, "Reed, if you don't eat and drink we will have to put you back in the hospital, and we don't want to do that. We know that you don't want to be there either." Then Mark asked Reed if he wanted him to fill up his cup with a drink. Mark told Reed that he didn't have to drink it all right then, but that his filling it up would be an indication that Reed was willing to at least try to eat and drink. Finally Mark gave Reed one minute to answer him. Reed didn't answer, so Mark stood up and said, "Well then, I'm relieved. Maybe the hospital can get some nutrition down you with a feeding tube." I was so sad. I knew Reed hated going to the hospital.

Mark started to get Reed undressed and ready for bed

when Reed told him to stop and just leave the room. Mark left the room very upset and sat out on the couch for an hour while his brother Clair (who was visiting) and I tried to coax Reed to take a few more bites of food and a few more swallows of drink. We made a little progress and finally went to sleep.

The next night, Reed felt somewhat better. Mark and Clair were so tired that I told them to go to bed and I would finish the night work. Mark turned back to Reed and said, "Reed, this is two nights in a row I'm being kicked out of your bedroom."

Reed gave his dad the biggest smile he'd had all day long, and with tears in his eyes said, "Dad, don't make a habit of it!"

Mark's heart melted as he gave Reed a big hug and kiss and said, "Reed, that's exactly what I needed to hear tonight. Whatever you do, please don't lose your sense of humor."

Later, Clair told Mark, "I don't know how you are doing this, but you are making the right decision. You're doing the right thing." Clair shook his head and continued, "I don't know how you are handling this. It's just too hard." He'd had no idea of the amount of work involved in our sons' care. Forcing Reed to eat was not a fun thing to do, but it was definitely the right thing to do.

The next morning Mark asked Rob what he wanted for breakfast. Rob said that he didn't want anything to eat, and we thought, "Oh no! Now we've got two sons who won't eat!"

Mark asked Rob what was going on, and he said, "Dad, I'm fasting for Reed." Mark was touched by Rob's love for Reed and his faith in God, but he cautioned Rob that although his intentions were good, he shouldn't fast from any medications he needed and he shouldn't fast for too long, because he needed to be careful of his own health, too.

Reed's not eating and drinking enough not only caused him to feel weak and sick, but it also caused his bowels to back up. After two enemas during his bowel routine, he finally got a few results. But the whole hydration thing wasn't just a one-meal or a one-day fix. It took weeks and weeks to build up Reed's reserves. At one point we took him to the emergency room to have his electrolytes checked to make sure he wasn't dehydrated, and he wasn't. However, we were disappointed to find out that he had a urinary tract infection (UTI).

While Reed was there at the hospital his thoracic doctor checked his trachea site and decided that Reed needed a larger-sized tube, which would require a third surgery. The hospital didn't have that size tube on hand and had to order it, so Reed and I had to go back a few days later. Reed had the surgery to insert the larger trachea tube, and we started all over again dealing with the air leak, his eating and drinking problems, his bowel issues, and of course, his pain.

When life gets you down, as it sometimes will,
And your face wears a frown 'cause you've had your fill
Of the challenges and trials day after day,
And you've 'bout given up, and you don't want to pray...

Then it's time to look inward and gather the strength
Of your spirit and soul....

From, Look Inward, Sheryl Nixon, 1996

Reed tried going back to school on January 16, 1996. However, the school bus that picked him up was so bouncy and rocked his chair so much that he didn't feel very well by the time he got to school. It was the last week of the semester and all of the students were taking tests, so Reed spent most of the time adjusting to being in his chair longer than usual and being out and about. He started his actual classes the following week.

I had a hard time with the schedule because we had so many nursing shifts that weren't filled that I had to do all of the morning work myself. On a no-nurse day I had to get Reed dressed and up in his wheelchair, fix and feed him breakfast, get myself ready for school, and go with him. By midday I was already exhausted. Then when school was out at 2:30 p.m. we had to hurry home for Reed's physical therapy appointment. Many times we had a doctor's appointment right after the therapy, so we didn't get home until 6:30 or later. I still had to fix dinner and clean up. I never felt like I had enough sleep and I was always tired.

Shortly after Reed returned to school he got very sick and was in the hospital for several months. Mark and I met with the school administration and decided that it would be best to have tutors for Reed at home instead of trying to get him to school. As a result, Reed went to school for only two weeks out of his entire senior year. The tutors came to our home and Reed was able to continue his education.

Reed had really enjoyed his marketing class at high school before the accident and had joined the marketing club, DECA. During his junior year at Algonquin, he had won first place in the state DECA competition, which qualified him for a four-day trip to St. Louis, Missouri, to attend the national competition. Unfortunately, Reed was injured after the state competition and was unable to go to nationals, so his cross-country teammate, close friend, and DECA club member went to St. Louis and gave Reed's presentation for him. It was recognized as one of the top ten best presentations in the nation that year.

Reed and Rob were blessed with exceptionally good minds and they were excellent students. Reed worked with his tutors to complete his senior classes to be able to graduate with his class. In his senior yearbook, each graduating senior was given ninety spaces to write whatever they wanted. After thanking his family and teammates Reed wrote: "Running is life. Go the extra mile." When I read this, I realized that Reed still had a big hole in his heart where athletics had been. I remembered a day during that year's track season when Reed seemed particularly down. When I asked him what was wrong he said, "There's a track meet after school today. I should be in the race." Although we didn't dwell on it, it was a reminder of all that he had lost.

Each time Reed was in the hospital, for whatever reason, he realized that having a spinal cord injury (SCI) was much more severe and life-changing than he had ever expected. He began taking an active part in learning about the medical field and how the human body functions. He needed to better understand, recognize, and receive the specialized care he required to stay healthy and keep his body prepared to accept any future advancement that might be found to improve his life.

CHAPTER **20**

OUR FIRST CHRISTMAS after the accident was both wonder-ful and heart-wrenching. As we tried to shop for the boys, we discovered some new, difficult realities that resulted from the accident. What do you buy for someone who can't move or do anything? Raelene was home for Christmas and helped me do the shopping. We looked and looked and finally decided to buy some shirts, music CDs, and treats for Reed and Rob, since the gifts we would normally have bought for them were impossible. Video games, running shoes, and other athletic equipment were out of the question.

Christmas Eve fell on a Sunday that year, so we were all getting ready for church when there was a knock at the door. When I opened the door, there stood Mitt and Ann Romney with their family, bearing gifts. Mitt was very busy with his family, political, and church responsibilities, so we were amazed that he and his family took the time to drive an hour to our house to bring love and cheer to all of us.

After church we were invited to have Christmas Eve din-ner with some of our best friends, the Hiers. There were four or five steps up into their house, so Maury arranged with an-other friend to use a spare door as a ramp for Reed and Rob to roll up into their house. The door worked great, and we all enjoyed a wonderful Christmas Eve dinner and evening to-gether. It was the first time Reed and Rob had been in anyone else's house since before the accident almost nine months before.

Christmas morning arrived completely different than any of us had ever experienced before. Instead of Natalie and Kent bounding into Mark's and my bedroom to wake us up, eager to get downstairs and open their presents, they found us both dressed and downstairs helping Reed and Rob get dressed and into their wheelchairs. It was nearly noon by the time we had everything ready to enjoy our Christmas morning. But our joy quickly turned to sorrow when we realized that neither Reed nor Rob could open their presents. Past Christmas mornings were spent hugging and kissing each other in gratitude for the generous gifts we shared, but since neither of our sons could move, we all went to them to show our appreciation.

We were nearly finished opening our gifts when we heard caroling outside. We opened the door and were surprised to see close to thirty people singing and carrying gifts and treats. With tears streaming down our faces, we welcomed each one into our home and thanked them for their love and for leaving their own Christmases to come and bring some happiness to us. It was an unforgettable experience that reminded us of the kindness and generosity of friends, neighbors, and people in general.

What will I give this Christmastime when so much has been given to me?
What will I sacrifice of mine so that others may receive?
My life has not been without trials, and sorrow I have seen.
And yet I've been so blessed because of love that's been given to me.

So what will I give this Christmastime, presents or money or toys?

What should I give to friends of mine to bring them the greatest joy?
Peace of heart. Peace of mind. Peace from worldly care.
Peace to make it through life's trials, peace is what I'd share....

From, What Will I Give This Christmastime,
Sheryl Nixon, 1998

♪♪♪♪

For two weeks straight in January we had at least one doctor's appointment every day. That doesn't sound so bad until you consider all of the time it took to get the boys loaded, to the doctor's office, and unloaded, and then loaded, back home, and unloaded again. Visits took us three hours by the time we got it all done. If we had two appointments then we were gone all day long. Reed and Rob had many doctors including dermatologists, podiatrists, neurologists, urologists, pulmonologists, physiatrists, endocrinologists, dentists, internists, infectious disease specialists, gastroenterologists, as well as their primary care doctors.

Reed always tried to be brave and not complain around his dad, and he somehow got it into his head that he was supposed to be that way around others, too. I frequently took Reed to the doctor or hospital and during those visits I'd tell the doctor all of the problems we were dealing with. But when the doctor turned to Reed and asked how he was doing, Reed usually replied, "Oh fine, not bad. Everything is going good."

Then as soon as we'd get loaded back up into the van Reed would start in, "Oh, I hurt all over. I don't feel good."

I was frustrated, feeling like a fool in front of the doctor, telling him all of the problems we faced one minute, just to have Reed say everything was fine the next minute. The doctor wasn't even aware of some of the issues we dealt with because Reed was "fine." I told Reed that he made me feel foolish when he said he was fine. He needed to be straightforward with his doctors if we were going to make any progress. He tried to do better at opening up to his doctors after that.

Even so, by the end of January 1996, Reed still wasn't feeling well. His air leak was still terrible and he was even having a difficult time talking, so I made an appointment with his pulmonologist. The doctor was not in because his wife had just delivered a baby, so Mark, Reed, and I met with two other doctors, one of them being the head of the pulmonology department at UMASS, to discuss what should be done to solve Reed's trachea tube air leak.

The department head thought that because Reed had lost so much weight he was being over ventilated (getting too much air during each breath), so he recommended lowering the tidal volume from 900 cc (cubic centimeters) per breath to 600 cc with 10 breaths per minute. He made the changes on the ventilator and Mark and I immediately saw that Reed was distressed. One-third of his air had just been taken away and he was really struggling to breathe.

The doctor also recommended keeping Reed's cuff inflated most of the time so that all of the air went into his lungs instead of some escaping through his mouth, but that meant that most of the time Reed wouldn't be able to speak! I looked at Reed, who was still grimacing in distress, and I was furious! Speaking was all Reed had left, and this doctor was going to take even *that* away! I wasn't about to take him home struggling to breathe like he was. It was easy enough for the doctor to say to do this and do that and send us home, but he didn't have to live with the pain and discomfort every hour of every day. The department head's recommendations were not acceptable, but he wouldn't listen to any suggestions, either from us or the other doctor. I didn't know what else to do, so I sat down and began to cry.

Mark and I were quietly talking about what we should do when the doctor said, "I want to see both of you out in the hall!"

Good grief! You'd have thought we were kids being disciplined at school the way he treated us. He was not willing to talk about the matter in front of Reed. In fact, he treated Reed as though he wasn't even there, and ignored the distress he was in.

That man was arrogant and patronizing to everyone. He behaved as though his way was the only way. We argued back and forth until he finally said that he had to go to a meeting. When he left Mark and me in the hall with the other doctor, we knew it was just an excuse for him to leave. He obviously wasn't used to anyone opposing him. Mark and I were Reed's advocates and we were not about to let some know-it-all doctor—head of the department or not—make rash and unreasonable decisions where Reed was concerned.

It was obvious to me that the head of the department's recommendations were made by the book without much, if any, consideration for Reed. He didn't seem to have any concern for how much discomfort Reed was feeling, physically or emotionally, and his bedside manner was cold and unsympathetic.

Mark and I continued talking with the other doctor, trying to come up with a reasonable solution. Finally I asked, "If the tidal volume has to come down, why can't it be done gradually, say maybe 100 cc per week instead of all at once? At least that would be more feasible than the immediate drop suggested." The doctor finally agreed to lower Reed's tidal volume gradually over three weeks' time. Why did I have to think of that? Shouldn't the doctors have had more than one option? I was thoroughly disgusted with those pulmonology doctors.

Mark, the other doctor, and I went back into Reed's room and told him the new plan while the doctor reset the ventilator. Reed was relieved that he could go home breathing comfortably. Over the next three weeks we lowered his tidal volume gradually until we reached the recommended 600 cc. Reed handled the gradual decrease of air just fine, and he felt much better than when his air was drastically reduced all at once.

One evening Mark stayed home with Reed while I went to see Natalie and Kent perform in their choir concert at school and Rob was on a date with his girlfriend. At one point Mark didn't think Reed was breathing quite right, so he decided to bag him (manually force air into his lungs with an AMBU bag) and Reed felt better. But the next evening by the time we all got home from church, Reed looked pretty bad, like someone had painted his face for Halloween: chalky white with dark circles around his eyes, charcoal lines by his mouth, and dark patches under his cheekbones. I had never seen someone look so near death.

The next day I was trying to feed Reed a couple of bites of food and a few sips of juice when all of a sudden his eyes fixed up toward his left in a weird stare and he grimaced. I asked him what was the matter and if he could breathe, but when he tried to answer his words came out as gibberish, nonsense. I immediately began bagging him, but when he didn't respond, I put the ventilator back on him and ran to call 911. I returned and kept bagging Reed until the paramedics arrived and took him to the hospital.

We waited several hours in the emergency room until Reed was finally admitted into the hospital. At that moment a tremendous weight was taken off my shoulders. I actually felt guilty because I was so relieved. Reed had been home from the hospital four and a half months, and the entire time he had been sick. Mark and I had done everything we could think of to help, but nothing had worked.

While Reed was in the hospital, the pulmonary doctors decided to change his trachea tube yet again and this time to check inside, above, and below the trachea site, to see if Reed's larynx and trachea were in good condition. But there was so much swelling that they couldn't see anything. They took Reed into the operating room and put him under general anesthesia so they could move the tissue aside and see what was going on. One of the doctors told me that when they looked at the trachea, the small square that was made during Reed's surgery in November had stretched out of shape and was now a large oval-shaped opening. No wonder Reed had been leaking so much air. To top it off, one of his lungs was collapsed.

Reed was scheduled to have trachea surgery on May 24 to remove three centimeters, or about 1 ¼ inch, of his damaged trachea at Mass General Hospital in Boston, with a doctor who supposedly "wrote the book" on tracheal reduction surgery. But that was four months away, and we had a lot to do to get him well enough for the surgery to be done.

Mark and I were afraid Reed might not live long enough to have the trachea surgery because he was so sick and had so many different health problems. Besides his trachea problems, he had an antibiotic-resistant (VRE) urinary tract infection (UTI), kidney stones that needed blasting with surgery, and lots of pain in his chest. Reed was put on a two-week regimen of IV antibiotics to clear up his UTI, but they weren't working very well.

Every day we hoped that Reed would be well enough

to come home from the hospital, but every day it seemed a different problem would arise: a CAT scan, pneumonia, or a collapsed lung. March 3 was Reed's eighteenth birthday and there he lay, stuck in the hospital. What a miserable way for Reed to celebrate the beginning of his adulthood. And what would that adulthood be like?

Reed's scheduled transfer to Fairlawn rehab hospital had to be postponed three times, and he ended up staying at UMASS for four weeks. There was one bright spot, though, during this discouraging time. At his scouting board of review (held at the hospital), Reed got a unanimous decision qualifying him for his Eagle Scout award. His Court of Honor was held May 11, and Reed became an Eagle Scout, the highest rank in the scouting program.

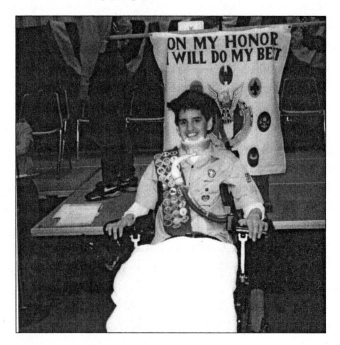

Reed receives Eagle

While Reed and I were there at the hospital, Reed's GI doctor spoke to us about our options for a feeding tube, and we decided to have a G-tube, which would go directly into Reed's stomach, similar to the one he had in the VA Hospital. Reed needed a lot more nourishment than he had been getting, and with a G-tube he would get all of the nourishment he needed without having to eat and drink through his mouth.

Reed's urologist also checked on him at the hospital and wanted him to have another sphincterotomy because his muscles were still holding in too much urine, causing frequent urinary tract infections. Lying there in the hospital, Reed was very sad and discouraged. He told me he was unhappy because "it isn't the same at school. The kids just say 'hi' and walk on by. I can't remember what it feels like to walk or run. I can't even remember how I did it."

He cried and cried, but because his cuff was inflated, not a soul could hear him. I desperately wanted to hold him in my arms to comfort and console him, but even if that had been possible, he wouldn't have been able to feel my warmth and tenderness. Reed mourned the loss of his youth and the loss of his body.

I tried to encourage Reed by challenging him to try to make other people happy. I told him a story by Janeen Brady that I remembered about a little princess who was very sad. Her father, the king, wanted her to be happy, so he gave her a magic box. The princess could wish for any outfit she wanted to wear, and when she opened the box, there it was! She was so happy!

But soon she had too many clothes and she was tired of new clothes. So the king gave his daughter a different magic box. This time all she had to do was wish for a toy and it would be there inside the box. Again, the princess was happy.

Soon, however, she had too many toys and she didn't know what to do with them all. She tried putting the toys back in the magic box and wishing them away, but that didn't work. She tried throwing them away, but there were just too many. She was very unhappy.

The princess' birthday was coming up and the king wanted his daughter to be happy, so he planned a big birthday party for her. The princess and her father decided to invite all of the children in the kingdom. At the party, the princess gave a toy to each of her guests. Everyone had a wonderful time and the princess discovered that the way to be happy was to make other people happy.

I suggested to Reed that perhaps he would be happier if he tried to make other people happy whenever he could, even though I realized he was mostly just trying to survive each day. Over the next several months I could tell that Reed was making an effort to make people happy. Many times when visitors left his room they told me, "I feel a lot better after talking to Reed. When I went into his room I didn't know what to say. He has really cheered me up!"

CHAPTER 21

ON JUNE 9, 1996, Reed reached his goal to graduate with his class and he rolled across the stage to receive his high school diploma. When Reed's name was read, everyone immediately jumped to their feet to give him a standing ovation. At that moment it wasn't just our family with tears rolling down our cheeks. Many people around us were overjoyed with Reed's accomplishment. This was a big pay-off day for many in our community who had supported Reed over the past year in countless ways.

What we didn't know at the time was that as each graduate crossed the stage, they carried a dollar bill in their hand and gave it to the principal when they shook his hand. Reed's entire graduating class contributed to this cash gift to him as a token of their admiration.

Reed's High School Graduation

By the time college was to begin that fall, Reed still wasn't well enough to attend, but in January of 1997, Reed entered Bentley University, the business university where his dad was a professor. I drove Reed to school and took notes for him until my friend Charlene took over for me so I could be home to help my other kids.

The first class we went to was a World Civilizations class. Since Reed couldn't take his own notes and I couldn't write down everything the professor said, I asked her if I could record the lecture so Reed could study at home. She said no because she would be too embarrassed knowing that she was being taped. Later, Reed and I learned that according to The Americans with Disabilities Act (ADA), she was required to let us record the class, but we didn't know it at the time. We still had a lot to learn.

College is challenging in and of itself, but Reed had a difficult time adjusting. First of all, it took us an hour to get to Bentley, unload, and get to class, so Reed was already tired when we got there. Then, because he was on such heavy medications, he often fell asleep. Sometimes he made sleeping sounds loud enough that I had to shake him to wake him up.

Sitting with Reed in class, I immediately recognized several challenges facing him that we would have to address. On the first day of class, the professor went through the syllabus for the semester. Reed's grade for the class would be determined by class participation, group projects, and tests and quizzes. Since he couldn't raise his hand to participate, I didn't know how he could possibly get a decent grade in the class. After discussing it, Reed and I decided that he would let me know if he had a comment or question and I would raise my hand for him.

I also recognized that because Reed didn't live on campus, getting together with other students for group work would be difficult. After a lot of planning, arranging, and rearranging schedules, the groups were able to get together to work on projects. Even so, Reed was diligent in his assignments when other students often slacked off. It was hard to strike a good balance between the students and the assignments.

Reed learned early on that communicating with his professors in regard to homework, papers, group work, and exams enabled him to be successful and enjoy college. When it came to tests or quizzes, Reed couldn't take them in class because he had to tell me the answers to write down and the other students would hear him. After talking to the professor about the problem, she suggested we go across the hall and take the exam in an empty room where we could talk out loud without disturbing anyone else. Eventually, many of Reed's professors trusted us enough to let Reed take the tests at home, saving us the two-hour travel time to campus and back.

Working through these challenges that first semester helped us through the rest of Reed's college experience.

❧❧❧❧

By the time our second Christmas had passed, Mark and I had worked so hard taking care of Reed and Rob day and night that we were worn out. We wondered how we had managed to survive for so long. Every day for the past year and a half Mark had done the night shift. There was a lot of work that needed to be completed before Reed and Rob were settled for the night.

It began with transferring them from their wheelchairs to their beds. After getting them undressed, giving them medications, and brushing their teeth, they each needed thirty minutes of range of motion exercises (repeatedly moving each joint in their arms, hands, legs, and feet) before being turned on their side and going to sleep. Mark seldom got to bed before 1:00 a.m.

Because each boy had to be turned on his opposite side every three hours (to avoid bedsores), Mark set his alarm for 4:00 a.m. and again at 7:00 a.m. In between turns he had the monitor on so he could hear Reed click or Rob call out if they needed help. After the 7:00 a.m. turn, the nurse came and Mark was able to jump in the shower to get ready for work. With only five hours of interrupted sleep, Mark still had a full day's work at Bentley University.

Friends and family often asked Mark, "How in the world are you able to keep this up?"

Mark replied, "There came a point early on where I felt like I hit a wall—physically, mentally, and spiritually spent. I realized I needed to be more specific in my prayers to God. Instead of asking for strength to make it through the night and day, I asked God to make each hour of my sleep count as if it were three. Then I trusted that He would hear my prayers. There was never any strength left at the end of the day, but I felt God strengthen me when I had nothing left. It was remarkable."

But after a year and a half of this grueling routine, Mark finally had to admit that he physically couldn't continue. When we first brought the boys home it never crossed our minds that we would wear out and need help. We decided we needed more than just the nurses during the day and evening hours; we needed help during the night, too. The previous month we had run an ad in the newspaper for a live-in personal care attendant (PCA) and had received quite a few responses, but most lacked the necessary skills to perform the job.

We finally hired our first live-in PCA. The woman was a very hard worker, but because she slept so soundly, she struggled to wake up to Reed's clicks and Rob's calling out to her during the night. She also had some difficulty handling some of the medical aspects of their care, such as suctioning Reed's lungs or performing range of motion on the boys' limbs. After five weeks we finally had to let her go.

We were blessed, however, to find a wonderful young woman who had recently graduated from Boston University in speech therapy and was working part time for another disabled individual. She had read about Reed and Rob in the featured article in the *Boston Globe Magazine* and called us to find out more about them. Mark and I offered the live-in position to her and she agreed to take the job.

Since hiring our first live-in PCA, we have had a total of seventeen different people live with us for various lengths of time. Every time a PCA has left for school or another job, finding someone new to take the position has been a difficult process. Whenever we needed a new PCA, we'd let our families and neighbors know, but that wasn't always a broad enough spectrum to find someone.

It took such an amazing amount of faith. We trusted that heaven would help us find someone to live with us if we were patient. I was often reminded of a scripture in the Bible, Proverbs 3:5-6 which says, "Trust in the Lord with all thine heart; and lean not unto thine own understanding. In all thy ways acknowledge him, and he shall direct thy paths."

Finally, Mark came up with a great idea for how to find PCAs more easily. Every year since our marriage we had sent a Christmas letter to all of our close friends and families. Mark suggested that we send information about the boys and the job opportunity to the people on our Christmas letter list.

Mark's idea was a life-saver for us. Since we started sending letters to our Christmas list, we have always been able to find someone to take the live-in position. Sometimes we only had one or two people to choose from, but other times we had a whole list. But hiring the person was only the beginning. Almost all of our live-in PCAs were totally inexperienced, so the training was pretty extensive.

Sometimes, however, training was the least of our PCA problems. Once in a while we had someone with us who was very difficult to live with. I'm sure that many times they thought we were pretty hard to live with as well. Generally speaking, we were able to deal with each other's quirks, but once I really clashed with a PCA. Before the PCA was hired I'd told my doctor that I thought my antidepressant medication made me feel too mellow, so he changed it. I didn't realize that the side effects of this new medicine made me particularly impatient, grumpy, and aggressive—not a good combination for our situation. As a result, I always seemed to be upset with our PCA. Unfortunately, he left our employment on a sour note, and I have always regretted that I didn't know of the medication's side effects until after he was gone. As a result of that sad experience, I got back on track with my antidepressants and I have not changed my medication since.

After finding someone to fill the live-in job, we still had to find a morning PCA to help the nurse get Reed showered and dressed. Mark and I usually asked around our community and at church for suggestions for interested people, and we've done pretty well in filling that part-time position. Over and over, we relied on the Lord to find people to work for us.

CHAPTER **22**

DURING THESE TRYING times I read an article written by Elaine Jack entitled "Grounded and Settled." In the article she gave an analogy that has stayed with me. A woman had been planning a trip to Italy for many years. In preparation, she studied the language and literature. All of her friends were planning trips to Italy, as well. Finally the day came when she boarded the plane and took off. But when she landed, the attendant announced, "Welcome to Holland."

"Holland?" she asked. "But I was supposed to go to Italy! All of my friends are in Italy. I don't want to be in Holland! I don't know the language or anything about Holland!"

But there she was and nothing could change that. After a while she began to notice that Holland had Rembrandts and windmills and tulips. She began to make friends with new people. In time, she learned to know and love many things about Holland.

And so it was with me. I had found myself in a completely different place than I'd ever thought, but there were many blessings I received from being there. The final thought in the article was, "If you spend your life mourning the fact that you didn't get to Italy, you may never be free to enjoy Holland."

I knew I needed to look for the blessings and choose to be happy. Otherwise I would never find the spiritual peace I was seeking so that I could enjoy the rest of my life.

I have been blessed with great faith in the Lord. Over and over again I have used that faith to call upon Him for help

through difficult trials, and each time I have been tremendously strengthened. I remember one particular night, shortly
after the accident, praying and saying, "Heavenly Father, I
can't do this anymore."

I was reminded of one of the Psalms in the Bible that says,
"Cast your burden upon the Lord and He will sustain thee."
(Psalms 55:22)

But then I thought, "Exactly how do I do that?" With no
answer to my question, I fell asleep. After a good night's sleep,
I woke up and somehow found the energy to make it through
another stress-filled day. I frequently felt the strength of the
Lord helping me, whether it was with something simple, like
remembering to make an appointment, or something difficult,
such as Reed's emergency visits to the hospital and trying to
figure out what was wrong. The more faith I showed in the
Lord, the more help I received, and I knew that I could count
on Him to get me through the hard times.

One of Reed's doctors, who was familiar with our family's
religion, asked Mark, "How has your faith been challenged,
and what struggles do you have regarding your faith?"

Mark thought for a moment and replied, "My faith is
stronger now than it was before the accident. It may have
been challenged, but the result has been that it has grown,
not diminished. The purpose of faith is to strengthen us when
challenges come, and I have felt that strength."

During an interview with a CNN reporter Mark was asked,
"Do you ever worry that this is going to get old?"

Mark replied, "It's old now."

Then the reporter asked, "Do you ever ask 'Why me?'"

"Why not me?" Mark replied. "Why should I be exempt
from trials? The accident wasn't a punishment. The Lord has
supported all of us in many ways. I don't believe any of our

family has ever asked, 'Why me?' Bad things happen to good people all the time. We all go through difficult times."

Mark and I decided not to be pulled into the unhappy world of self-pity, but rather to do our best to serve others, have faith, and trust in our Father in Heaven. After all, Reed and Rob were alive! We were blessed during our deep sorrow. Somehow we were able to understand that happiness was a choice, and we chose to be happy.

Every mornin' I wake up and stumble out of bed
Lookin' for some aspirin to soothe my achin' head.
The night before I wondered how I'd face another day.
But here I am this mornin' just tryin' to find my way.

I never did consider what I'd ever do
If my life turned upside down, how would I get through?
Would faith and hope help me survive? 'Cause I could not turn back.
Or would I get discouraged and maybe start to ask

Why me? Why me? Would I then begin to ask
Why me? Why me? Life is so unfair.

When I look at others and their adversity
Many live with sorrow, and some have known defeat.
And so I have to tell myself, I am not alone,
'Cause people all around the world have troubles of their own....

From, Why Me, Sheryl Nixon, 2006

People often wondered how our marriage was holding up. Mark and I were at Maury and Charlene Hiers' home one evening when they asked us, "How are you holding things together? Should we be worried about your marriage?"

Mark said, "You know, I guess our marriage could fall apart, but I've just been too busy watching out for Sheryl, and she relies on my suggestions. When you have someone who trusts you, you have to be very careful what you say. I try to be sensitive and only make suggestions I am confident are correct."

A good example of Mark's watching out for me happened one night at midnight when Natalie suddenly informed me that she needed a paper typed right away so she could turn it in the next day at school. It was already way past my bedtime and I was exhausted, but I felt obligated to do the typing since I was seldom home to help her. Mark found out about it and put his foot down telling Natalie that she would have to turn in her handwritten copy. I felt as if I'd let her down again, but Mark knew how badly I needed sleep in order to make it through the next day.

I told Maury and Charlene that for most of our married life Mark and I have had "date night" every Friday evening. We loved spending time together, and it was important for us to remember why we married each other in the first place.

I love your tender care. I love it when you brush my hair. And all the time you share with me. And when I'm feeling blue, I know that I can lean on you. And sometimes, you cry, too, with me.

You're all that I want, everything that I need And more, much more than I deserve. Every day when I awake, I know there's no mistake You're more, much more than I deserve....

I love you. Oh, how I love you. You love me, too.
From, More Than I Deserve, Sheryl Nixon, 1984

After the accident we found it even more important to have those dates. They helped us to be strong as a unit, and if we could be united together, we could help our family be strong and united, too. Therefore, instead of falling apart, we pulled together. Date nights saved us.

Something else helpful was that Mark and I were able to allow each other to grieve in our own way. Since I was on medication for depression, my emotions were relatively steady and I didn't cry very much. However, Mark reacted differently. He cried a lot. It tore him apart to watch his sons suffer so much at such an early age and not be able to help them or take away their pain. It was also very hard for Mark to be at work all day long; he was able to see Reed and Rob only a few hours each night. He was really emotional, but that didn't bother me, and my lack of emotion seemed okay with him.

Next, our friends asked if we had noticed any changes in our personal lives. Mark explained, "I've had an opportunity to evaluate my life. Now I have more energy and commitment to make changes. I think I'm a better person for it."

I added, "We've had to make a conscious choice not to be bitter and angry. In the midst of life's trials, you can choose to be happy."

❧❧❧

Reed, Rob, and our family continued to be blessed by the love and generosity of other people. Mark's colleagues at Bentley University decided to put together a fundraiser to earn enough money for us to buy a new handicap-accessible van for the boys to go to and from their college classes at Bentley, and the school donated $3,000 to set up the event.

Hoping to raise $40,000, the faculty at Bentley joined together and scheduled a 5K run/walk, a banquet, and a silent auction to benefit our family. If enough items were donated, there would also be a live auction.

The morning of the race I got up early, got dressed, and left to pick up Reed, who was still in the hospital. I was running a little late, so by the time Reed and I got back home to pick up the other kids and leave for Bentley, it was already 9:15. It was a good forty-minute drive to campus, and the race was supposed to start at 10:00! Four of the boys' friends who were going to run in the race followed me to Bentley, so I was not only worried about making *them* late, but I had the two guests of honor with me!

Mark left for Bentley early that morning to help set everything up, so he was already there and on the bullhorn lining everyone up to begin the race when we pulled up, barely five minutes before the gun went off. I stopped right there at the starting line and got Reed and Rob out of the van. Rob planned on participating in the race, so without a second to spare he quickly rolled over to the starting line and took off with an early lead. I had to be at the end of the race to take pictures, so Reed and I hurried across campus as fast as we could. We barely made it there before the first runner came in. It was really hectic, but everyone enjoyed participating.

The banquet and auction were to be held that evening. There wasn't much time for the boys to rest in between the events, but the night was a wonderful success. Mark, Reed, and Rob each spoke for a few minutes and I sang two of my songs. Following the banquet, a live auction was held with a Bentley faculty member as the auctioneer. He did a fabulous job, even changing his hat several times and doing everything possible to introduce each item in a new and exciting way. It was obvious that people had come planning to spend money, because nearly every item went for more than the previously determined minimum bid.

The hottest item of the auction was a set of four tickets to a Red Sox baseball game. Four professors got together and decided to pool their money so they could bid high enough to win the tickets. Somehow the department chair caught wind of their plan and started bidding against them just to raise the price. He finally let the professors take the bid at $775! We were all laughing and cheering along with everyone else there. A few people didn't win anything they bid on, but they made donations anyway.

The auction was followed by a dance with a DJ. Mark was on the ballroom dance team in college, so he took turns dancing with his daughters and me. Rob was even out on the dance floor rolling around with his girlfriend sitting on his lap. People really got a kick out of that. We all had so much fun that Reed didn't get back to the hospital until 1:00 a.m.! In the end over $60,000 was raised, enough for a new van and gas for a year!

CHAPTER 23

MARK AND I had not tried traveling with Reed and Rob other than by car until our oldest daughter, Raelene, got married in Utah on December 19, 1996. Our second daughter, Renae, was married in Utah in August 1995, but Reed and Rob were unable to attend, since they were both still in the VA Hospital. They had been home well over a year when Raelene announced her engagement and wedding, and since our friend, Craig Donaldson, had given Reed and Rob airline tickets, we decided to give flying a try.

It took a tremendous amount of work to travel with disabled teenagers, especially if the trip required flying. I believe most people would avoid air travel altogether if they took a disabled person with them. However, most of our family lived out West and we knew they would want us to visit them. I had an experience in my first year of marriage that helped me decide that Reed and Rob should be able to travel more than just by car if they wanted to.

In 1975, shortly after Raelene was born, I learned that my high school boyfriend was in the hospital with encephalitis (brain disease) as a result of a mosquito bite, and he was in a coma. Many months later, when he came out of the coma, he had problems on the left side of his body, making it difficult for him to walk or speak very well. He tried a semester of college, but it just didn't work out for him. Since that time, he has spent most of his life staying at home.

When Reed and Rob were injured I was determined for

them to experience life—including air travel. They were very young and had their whole lives ahead of them. I refused to limit Reed and Rob because of my fears and inabilities, so I worked hard to learn how to make air travel possible for them.

With Reed's and Rob's tickets on American Airlines, we bought a ticket for Mark to fly with them. I had some available sky miles on Delta Airlines that I used for Natalie's, Kent's, and my tickets, so we were split up on two different airlines. First, we all flew to Salt Lake City for the wedding and reception. We held a second reception in College Station, Texas, and a third reception back home in Northborough. It was a significant amount of traveling and having never traveled with two paralyzed sons before, we had no idea what to expect. Wow. It was certainly a lesson in what we should have done and what we should never do again!

Mark and the boys were allowed to board the plane first. Mark worked incredibly hard because no one else knew how to help him. Getting Rob on the plane wasn't too bad. First, Rob had to be lifted out of his wheelchair and put into an aisle chair that was narrow enough to roll onto the plane and down the center aisle. Then he was lifted out of the aisle chair and into his assigned seat on the plane. That was a lot of work, but because Rob didn't weigh too much, Mark was able to handle it by himself.

Reed was an entirely different story. It took a half dozen airport employees to help Mark get Reed onto the plane. Like Rob, Reed had to be lifted into an aisle chair, rolled onto the plane, and lifted into his seat. But when Reed was lifted in and out of the chairs, he had to wear a cervical collar to support his neck and have his hands tied together so that his arms wouldn't fall.

The main difficulty Mark faced with Reed was that Reed

couldn't breathe on his own and had to use an AMBU bag when he wasn't hooked up to the ventilator. Mark and several employees lifted Reed into the aisle chair. Another employee was in charge of the AMBU bag that breathed for Reed until Mark could get the ventilator off of the wheelchair, onto the plane, and hooked up to Reed. While Reed was being lifted, someone else grabbed his seat cushion from his wheelchair and handed it to an attendant to put down where he would be sitting. When Reed was finally in his seat, his neck and chest had to be tied to the back of the seat, so he wouldn't fall forward.

When Reed was finally settled, Mark had to take the arm, foot, and head rests off the wheelchair, put them in a box, disconnect the two batteries, put them each in their own box, and then send the wheelchair with an airport employee to put in the belly of the plane with the rest of the luggage.

One big problem occurred when Mark realized that all three of their seats were three-quarters of the way back on the plane. The rows were really close together, making it very difficult to lift Rob over to the window seat and Reed to the center seat. Mark had to sit on the aisle so that he could help the boys during the flight. Finally, after the three of them were situated, the rest of the passengers were allowed to board the plane.

The layover in Cincinnati, Ohio was another problem. Mark, Reed, and Rob had to wait until all of the passengers deplaned before they could begin the process of getting off. The wheelchairs had already been transferred to the next flight, so Reed and Rob had to be lifted onto an electric cart to be taken to the next gate. By the time all three of them got there, the passengers for the next flight were already on board. Transferring the boys with all of the passengers already in their seats meant that there weren't any empty rows to climb over or seats to lay equipment on. With everyone watching, Mark was terribly uncomfortable, and by the time he had the boys settled in their seats he was completely exhausted. In the end the flight was forty-five minutes late taking off.

When the plane landed in Salt Lake City and the wheelchairs were brought to the door, Raelene's fiancé, Mark Norman, helped Mark get Reed and Rob transferred into their wheelchairs. But when Reed tried to drive his chair with his TTK, the chair didn't work. The baggage handlers hadn't been careful enough and something was broken. It was a good thing Mark Norman was strong enough and able to push, because Reed and his wheelchair together weighed almost four hundred pounds and Mark Nixon was way too exhausted from the flights to push that much weight.

At that point in time there weren't any handicap-accessible vans to rent unless we paid for a driver as well, so we used my mom and dad's camper van to get Reed from the airport to the hotel. Their van wasn't big enough for both boys in their wheelchairs, so Rob was lifted onto the seat of Mark Norman's truck, and the luggage was loaded in the back.

Natalie, Kent, and I arrived an hour or so before the guys, so we went to the hotel and checked in. I had previously arranged with the management to have two rooms. One of them was to be a handicap-accessible room with two single beds and a roll-in shower. When we arrived, however, the accessible room had a king-sized bed, and a bathroom with a tub and grab bars instead of a roll-in shower.

Mark and I had to be able to work with Reed from both sides of the bed, so it was impossible to put him on the king-sized bed. At home Reed slept on an air mattress to reduce the risk of bedsores, and we brought the mattress with us, so we put it on the floor for Reed to sleep on and Rob slept in the bed. It was really hard taking care of Reed on the floor. There were tubes, power cords, and pieces of equipment all around, making it practically impossible to maneuver around him. Once or twice his trachea tube really got yanked, which was very painful for Reed. For the next several days Mark was on the phone with two different companies until he finally got the wheelchair working again.

The wedding and reception were wonderful, but short-lived, because the very next morning we flew to Texas for Raelene's second reception. Only smaller airplanes fly into College Station because it isn't a very big airport, so in Dallas/Fort Worth, Reed, Rob, and Mark had to change from American Airlines to American Eagle. It sounded great when we booked the flight, but getting Reed and Rob on that small plane was almost impossible. All of the other passengers waited on the tarmac while Mark got Reed and Rob on the plane.

Everyone was on board and ready to go, when the pilot came to tell Mark that he'd been informed that the plane wasn't approved to carry an LP6 (Reed's type of ventilator) and Reed and Rob might have to change planes. After all the work it had taken to get them on the plane, Mark was not about to take them off, so he said, "Well, call the tower back and get approval!" After that issue was resolved, some of the passengers had to change seats because the weight of the wheelchairs was causing an imbalance in the cargo hold. The plane finally took off—late again.

In College Station an airport employee brought a lift with Rob's wheelchair up to the door of the plane. Mark got Rob transferred into the aisle chair, rolled him to the door, and transferred him into his wheelchair. The lift lowered Rob to the ground, and then Reed's wheelchair was brought up to the door to load him in. With the help of several employees, Mark was able to get Reed into the aisle chair. But while one of the employees held Reed's ventilator and Mark pushed Reed toward the door, the ventilator alarm went off. Mark asked Reed if he was breathing and he indicated that he wasn't, so Mark quickly, but calmly, asked for the AMBU bag (so as not to frighten the airline attendants), which was still back with the equipment where the boys had been sitting. As Mark immediately began bagging Reed, the attendant breathed a sigh of relief, "Okay, now we've got him breathing!"

Mark was still bagging Reed as he rolled him to the door and got him transferred into his wheelchair. Then the ventilator was hooked up to the chair battery and Reed was able to breathe with it again. When the lift operator asked Mark how much Reed and the wheelchair weighed and Mark told him about four hundred pounds, the operator, who was also on the lift, said, "We may exceed the maximum weight recommendations." But after considering the options (there weren't any), he finally said, "Well, let's just try it."

When the guys were all safely on the ground and Reed tried to drive his wheelchair, it was broken again. Mark tried wiggling the wires around to make sure they were all plugged in, and after thirty minutes he finally got it going again.

When we arrived at Mark's brother Clair's house for the reception, we had forgotten that there were several short steps to get inside. Clair hurried out to his garage to scrounge up some wood for a makeshift ramp. He found the wood, and Reed and Rob were able to get inside. The reception in Texas was very nice. Reed and Rob really enjoyed seeing many of their old friends. After the evening's festivities were over and the boys went down the makeshift ramp, the boards cracked. Fortunately they made it onto the sidewalk okay and we got them back to our hotel. But if Mark and I had known how much work it would be, we would never have taken Reed and Rob to the Texas reception.

Fortunately, Mark had the good sense to change his and the boys' airline tickets so that they didn't have to fly on another small commuter plane on their return flight. Instead, after recruiting several cousins for the two-hour drive to Austin to get Reed and Rob loaded on the plane, they took a non-stop flight back to Boston. That way they were able to avoid both the small plane as well as the layover with its change of planes. Mark vowed never again to travel alone with Reed and Rob. It was just too much work for one person.

As a result of that trip, Mark and I decided we would always travel together—no matter what. Next, if it was available, we would always fly non-stop, even if it was more expensive. Having to change planes was brutal. We single-handedly destroyed the airline's on-time statistics for the entire year! We also learned that we needed to reserve the first row bulk-head seats, because it was just too hard to get Reed and Rob into their seats with rows in front and behind them. Finally, we learned to pack up Reed's wheelchair very carefully and emphasize to the baggage handlers the importance of being careful with it. It was extremely fragile, and if it broke Reed wouldn't be able to do anything on our vacation.

After hearing of our difficult flying experience with the boys, many of our friends wondered if we'd ever fly with Reed and Rob again. But we were very determined. We knew after our first trip that traveling with the boys was only possible if we planned ahead and were willing and able to do the work required.

One year we planned a Nixon Family reunion in Southern California. Several days before our trip, Reed began having a lot of muscle spasms in his neck and back with no particular reason for them. The spasms were more annoying than painful, so we went ahead with our travel plans. Because our previous live-in PCA had returned to school and we hadn't found a replacement yet, Mark and I had to travel with Reed by ourselves. Knowing it would be a lot of work, we took extra help with us to the Boston airport to get Reed loaded.

Unfortunately, the non-stop flight we had previously scheduled was canceled, and we ended up having to change planes in Salt Lake City, causing a huge amount of extra work for Mark and me, and a great deal of stress and strain on Reed.

Mark and I weren't strong enough to lift Reed out of his assigned seat on the plane and into the airplane's aisle chair by ourselves, so we had to get help from some of the airport employees. One of them was a large man who said he was confident he could lift Reed from his seat by himself, and we knew he could. But when he got his arms around Reed and heaved him up to lift him over into the aisle chair, Reed was lighter than the employee expected and he jammed Reed's head into the overhead luggage compartment! I stood there aghast! Reed was so fragile that I felt certain he had been injured. After getting Reed back into his wheelchair and on the ventilator again, we asked him if he'd been hurt during the transfer. Amazingly, he said he thought he was okay. In his usual positive attitude Reed told us that he considered the annoying muscle spasms before our trip to be a blessing from God, because they stiffened up his neck and back to the point that when they were jammed he wasn't injured. We had witnessed a miracle.

After a wonderful reunion we flew back to Salt Lake City and then on home to Boston. Our youngest son, Kent, was on our same flight to Salt Lake City and helped us get Reed off the plane and onto our connecting flight. Mark and I were very tired and we couldn't have made the change without him.

Traveling continues to be an interesting challenge. One of our recent trips out West was especially memorable. When we got to the airport in Portland, Oregon (after a family reunion there) the security guard wanted Reed to go through the metal detector in his wheelchair! We tried to explain to him that practically the whole wheelchair was metal. Besides, it was way too big to fit through the space provided. The guard eventually took Reed into a special screening area, patted him down, and checked every square inch of his wheelchair. The rest of us had already been through the checkpoint and were watching Reed from a distance. Mark noticed that the security guard was wiping a white collection cloth over Reed's arms, hands, legs, feet, and wheelchair checking for explosives.

Mark said, "Look at that crazy guy checking Reed's hands for explosives! Does he think Reed is faking it or something?"

Imagine our surprise when the security guard came to us and said, "Your son tested positive for explosives."

"What explosive?" I asked.

"Nitroglycerin," he replied.

For a moment we were all baffled. Then a light went on for me. "Oh, I know why," I explained. Sometimes Reed's blood pressure gets pretty high and we have to put nitro paste on his chest to bring his blood pressure down. We had to put some on him the night before last and the nitro has gone through the pores of his skin, so I'm sure the explosive reading is from that."

The guard was surprised and said, "This is the first true positive we have ever gotten."

I wanted to say, "Yeah, and you caught a quadriplegic!"— but I didn't. Then we had to fill out a lot of paperwork and

Reed had to be checked all over again. Fortunately we had arrived at the airport early enough to still make our flight on time. When we landed in Salt Lake City, we were the last ones off the plane, as usual. We were afraid we'd miss our connecting flight to Boston, so I asked one of the airport employees to call our next flight and ask them to hold the plane for us.

He said, "They can't hold the flight."

"Oh yes they can!" I assured him. "They've done it before and we need it now!"

I explained that all of Reed's supplies were in the belly of that plane. I told him that I wasn't going anywhere without those supplies. Without them, we couldn't take care of Reed. If we couldn't take care of him, he'd have to go to a hospital, and if he was in a hospital, well, we all knew what a mess that would be. The flight was held for us.

For the most part, people were very kind and helpful to us, but once in a while we were really surprised at how rude someone was.

One summer Mark and I took our whole family, six of us plus a PCA, out to Utah for Raelene's graduation from Brigham Young University (BYU). As was so often the case, when Reed's wheelchair was brought to us after we landed in Utah, it was broken. We finally got it working again and really enjoyed the week we all spent together with Raelene and Mark, and Renae and Jeff, who were also attending BYU at the time.

On our way home Mark and I were very concerned that Reed's chair would be damaged on the flight, so I asked the gate attendant if either Mark or I could follow the wheelchair down to the cargo hold to make sure it was handled with care when it got loaded. The gate agent didn't think that was possible, but I begged him to try to get permission for us. At that moment a man walked by in the opposite direction and said, "You're not going to get permission!" I had no idea who the man was and I couldn't believe that he was so rude to us when he didn't even know the situation.

Well, I later found out that the man was the pilot for our flight, so I was very surprised that he hadn't even introduced himself and had treated us so unkindly. Even the gate attendant told me that he was shocked at the pilot's behavior. Apparently, the pilot was already upset because of a last-minute gate change, which had caused his plane to arrive late. So when he got off his previous flight and saw that our family was going to make his next flight even later than it would already have been, he took his frustrations out on us.

Once we were all situated on the plane, the pilot came to our seats and told Mark and me to chill out and quit causing trouble. We stood up as Mark tried to explain our concerns because of the previous damage to Reed's wheelchair from being loaded improperly, and that on other flights we'd taken he had been allowed to go down to the cargo hold and assist in loading Reed's wheelchair. The pilot refused to listen to any discussion and said that if we continued to argue he would have us removed from the plane. Furious, Mark told the pilot that there had better not be any damage to Reed's wheelchair when the attendant brought it to us in Boston. Then we sat down in our seats and tried to calm down.

Mark turned to me and said, "I'd like to see them try to get Reed and Rob off this plane. If they even tried, I'd get on the phone and call a news reporter. It would be a great photo opportunity and story: "Pilot Drags Quadriplegics off Plane!" Unfortunately, I was angry during the whole flight back to Boston. When the plane finally landed and the pilot came out of the cockpit I went up to him with a paper and pencil to write down his name.

He saw me and said, "Here, let me spell it for you so you can get it right!"

Before we left, both the flight attendant and the gate agent gave me their names and said they would be happy to write letters to their head office explaining how rudely the pilot had treated us. Fortunately, when we got off the plane Reed's wheelchair worked.

The next day I called the corporate offices of Delta Airlines and told the customer service representative our experience, complete with names and spellings. We were compensated with seven future travel vouchers. We have since flown on Delta many times and haven't had any major problem.

We have taken a lot more trips over the past sixteen years, and every time we go we learn something new, because on nearly every trip some major issue comes up. We have gotten better at traveling, whether by vehicle or plane, but it's always a tremendous effort. Our best flight ever was when the plane was only half full and we were all bumped up to first-class seats. It spoiled us forever!

Over the many years since the accident, as a result of our learning how to travel with our sons by air, they have traveled with us to twenty states and Canada, but we're still learning how to make traveling easier, faster, and less stressful.

Another difficult time we had dealing with rude people was when *Jurassic Park: The Lost World* was at the theater and Reed and Rob were excited to see it on opening night. I bought the tickets that morning, and we planned to leave at 6:00 p.m. But just as we were ready to leave, Reed needed to have his lungs suctioned and we didn't get off until 6:20. The theater was already crowded, so I ran up the stairs to the handicap-accessible seating. All of the seats were filled with able-bodied people, so I ran down to the additional accessible seating at the bottom of the theater. Able-bodied people were sitting there, too.

I explained our situation to the three people sitting there hoping they would find other seats that were still available, but they just looked at me as if to say, "So what?"

I was really caught off guard. In the entire time since the accident, people had been kind, even going out of their way to make tough situations easier for us. An usher asked if he could help me, so I explained the problem to him. He went over to the people in the handicap seating and asked them to move. They finally got up and found seats closer to the screen than they had wanted.

I went over and said, "Oh thank you very much!"

One of them replied, "You're NOT welcome!"

I was taken aback for a moment and then tried to explain that it was really hard to get two quadriplegic sons to the movie on time. The lady scowled at me and said, "Then you should leave earlier!"

I returned to our seats and just stood there, amazed at what had just occurred. Natalie, a peacemaker at heart, saw what had happened and went over to the rude lady and told her how hard it was to get her brothers to the theater. The lady growled, "Then leave them home!"

When Natalie tried to respond, the lady plugged her ears.

At first I was shocked. Then I was angry. Then I just sat down and cried. I felt horrible. I actually tried to think of what Jesus would have done, but I just couldn't come up with anything. The kids all enjoyed the movie, but the whole time I sat there, hashing it out in my mind until I was fuming.

At home I prayed for help calming down. I even asked for forgiveness for anything I might have done wrong, but when

I went to bed that night I couldn't sleep. After a while I began mentally singing some hymns, and I finally fell asleep.

The next morning I felt a little better. I began wondering what I would do if anything like that ever happened again. I must admit that I considered saying, "A movie is being filmed about our sons, and I would like your names so that I can make sure you get the credit for being the rudest people we have ever met!" But after some reflection I decided I would simply say, "I'm sorry you don't understand, but thank you anyway." That was going to be hard to do. When I thought about it, I realized that we had actually been blessed *not* to have had more incidents like that one. Perhaps if it ever did happen again, I would be less shocked and more prepared with a kind response.

> I watched Him from a distance, the one they called the teacher.
> And as I drew near Him I heard, "Do ye even as I...."
>
> I saw Him forgive the sinner. With great compassion He led.
> To the sad heart, He was comforter. Unto us all He said,
> "Do ye even as I. For then ye shall receive
> All the blessings Father hath for those who follow me...."
>
> He sacrificed more than we comprehend.
> He asked only our heart in return.
> He gave up His life, as was prophesied.
> He was the chosen one.
>
> He showed me what I could be....
> He said, "Do ye even as I."
>
> *From, Do Ye Even As I, Sheryl Nixon, 1990*

CHAPTER **24**

BACK IN THE early years following the accident, Rob really suffered from frequent and severe muscle spasms, which are common in people with spinal cord injuries (SCI). He took Baclofen (an anti-spasmodic medication) and Valium (a muscle relaxant) to keep the spasms in check, but a strong side effect of the Baclofen and Valium was drowsiness. One of Rob's long-term goals was to be able to drive a car, and to achieve that goal he had to minimize his spasms and still be alert.

After discussing the problem with his doctors, Rob decided to have a Baclofen pump surgically implanted just under the skin of his abdomen. The pump would deliver the Baclofen directly to his spinal column instead of traveling throughout his bloodstream. Therefore his dose could be decreased from 140,000 micrograms (mcg) a day to 400 micrograms (mcg) a day (an incredible drop) and he would stop taking the 40 milligrams of Valium.

The pump was the size of a hockey puck and was implanted about six inches to the right of Rob's belly button. Since he was fairly skinny, the pump was quite noticeable when he wasn't wearing a shirt. Rob seldom went without a shirt though, so it really didn't matter to him.

03/21/2011

Baclofen pump

During the surgery, the doctor ran a tube just under the skin from the Baclofen pump, around Rob's waist, and directly into the spinal column in his back. After the operation Rob was in a lot of pain. In fact, he had a hypersensitivity to the pain: he could hardly move, let alone sit in his wheelchair. His vertical back incision rubbed right on his backbone, adding to his pain. I brought him home, but I had to take him back to the hospital a few days later to get help with his pain management.

The week after returning to school, Rob stayed late to finish up some homework assignments and called to ask me to pick him up, which I did. Unfortunately, when we were just about home, as I turned left onto our street, another car jumped the gun from the stop sign and ran into us, hitting the driver's side rear fender and knocking Rob's head against the side of the van. I was uninjured, so I called 911 on my cell phone, and Rob was taken by ambulance to the hospital. Since the van was still drivable, I followed closely behind.

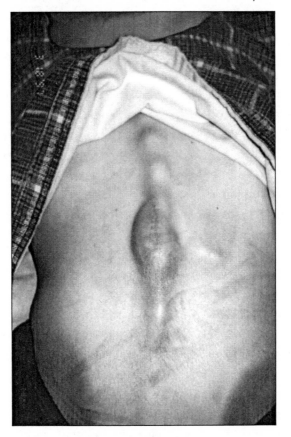

Rob's spinal fluid bubble

Rob had some tingling in his neck, so an x-ray was taken. The film looked normal and I took him home. The next day, however, Rob's PCA noticed a large bump on Rob's lower back that looked like a big blister. The PCA forgot to tell Mark or me, though, so the following day as I helped Rob get dressed, I saw the bubble, now about the size of a large egg, directly over the incision on his lower back. I called the doctor, who told me to watch it for a couple of days. When nothing changed, I took Rob in to have it checked. The doctor drained 6 cc of spinal fluid from the bubble and sent us back home. Several hours later the bubble had filled up again, so I called the doctor back. Apparently, the jolt from the car accident had torn some of the tubing of Rob's Baclofen pump loose, and his spinal fluid was leaking and causing the bubble on his back.

Rob needed a second surgery to patch the leak, so I took him to UMASS the next day, where the doctor performed a fluoroscopy (dye injected into the tubing for the Baclofen pump) to find the leak and patch it. Following the procedure, Rob was taken to "short stay" for observation for a couple of hours before he could go home.

I sat next to Rob's bed. The first hour and a half passed without any problems. Then, about a half hour before we were supposed to go home, Rob told me he was hot. I took his temperature, and instead of running in the low 97s as it usually did, it was in the high 97s. Then Rob told me that he had blurry, double vision. I got the nurse and she took Rob's temperature. It was 98.6, but I thought Rob felt much warmer than that. Something didn't feel right to me, so I stood up to check on him every few minutes.

Pretty soon I noticed that Rob was getting very drowsy. When he took a breath, his chest rose but then jerked near the end of the breath. I was sure something was wrong, and I got the nurse again. She tried to awaken Rob, but she couldn't. She took his vital signs and discovered his blood pressure had dropped to 90/40 and his heart rate was dropping, as well. She immediately called the doctor, who came right away and checked Rob.

The doctor told me that during the surgery he had tried to aspirate (extract) the fluoroscopy dye from the tube, but he couldn't get it out, so he had flushed the tube with Baclofen; otherwise it would have taken days for the dye to make its way through Rob's system and be replaced with Baclofen. Apparently that was standard procedure for able-bodied people, but Rob wasn't able-bodied, he was a quadriplegic. So when the doctor flushed the tube, Rob received an overdose of Baclofen. An anesthesiologist immediately came into the "short stay" room and administered the antidote for Rob's overdose. It must have really stung, because he woke right up. He was surprised that the two hours had passed so quickly and wondered why he was hooked up to so many tubes and wires.

I explained as Rob was transferred to the Immediate Care Area (ICA) of the hospital and got settled in. After about ten minutes Rob told me he was thirsty, so I got him some apple juice. He took a couple of sips and fell asleep again. When I told the nurse, she called the doctor, who told her that the antidote lasted only five to ten minutes and that she needed to administer a different medication whenever she was unable to wake Rob up.

Mark came to the hospital that evening to see how Rob was feeling and was surprised how "out of it" he was. I tried to wake him up, but it wasn't working very well. Rob was calling me Grandma, and when I pointed to Mark and asked who he thought Mark was, he sleepily replied, "Guy."

Rob finally woke up a little bit, and Mark and he visited for a while before Mark went home, exhausted after a long day at work.

There was a nursing shift change at 11:00 that night, so I met the incoming nurse and said goodbye to Rob's prior nurse. It is customary during a shift change for the nurses to meet and "report" or update the new nurse on the patient's condition. At 12:15 in the morning Rob began feeling uncomfortable. I closely watched the monitor detailing his decreasing vital signs: blood pressure still low and heart rate down from over sixty beats per minute to thirty-three. I hadn't seen a nurse since the shift change over an hour before. As I sat there alone with Rob a startling thought ran through my head: "What would I do if his heart stopped beating?"

I blinked.

Then Rob started tossing and said, "Mom, I'm going to throw up!" I quickly turned him on his side so he wouldn't choke on his vomit and I pushed the nurse's call button. No one answered.

I waited several seconds and then called out, "Nurse!" No one came, and Rob threw up all over the bed. Again I called out, "Nurse!" Still no one came. I yelled for a nurse a third and a fourth time and no one came. By that time Rob was not only vomiting, he was having diarrhea at the same time, and still no one answered the call button at the front desk.

Finally, a nurse came running in. I was furious! In the process of my chewing her out, she said, "We were in report."

I shouted, "What's more important, the patient or report?" When she hesitated at the question, I went ballistic, "Oh, report is more important is it?"

By that time, a nurse's voice from the front desk came on the loud speaker, "Can I help you?"

"Well it's about time!" I screamed back at her.

I was so upset that I didn't know what to do, so I called Mark and told him what had happened. He told me to put the head nurse on the phone. When she was on, he said, "This is Dr. Mark Nixon." After all he *is* a doctor—of accounting.

After discussing his concerns with the nurse Mark said, "If Sheryl has to call me one more time some heads are going to roll."

Rob's care was much better the rest of the night.

After several hours the crisis had passed, and Rob began to feel better. He was in the ICA for three days and came home the night before his eighteenth birthday. He spent that day lying flat in bed hoping to avoid another surgery, but when he got up in his wheelchair that evening, the spinal fluid bubble was still there. Rob was terribly disappointed. After all he'd been through, he was going to have surgery again after all.

Since Rob wasn't easily discouraged, however, he went into the surgery with a positive attitude. Following his recovery, he went back to school and never had a problem with the Baclofen pump again.

✦✦✦

Rob was determined to go to college after high school, so in preparation he took the SAT exam. He applied for and received a disability waiver that allowed him unlimited time to take the test. However, the accommodation didn't do him any good because the teacher who was assigned to help him wasn't familiar with the math. When Rob described the procedures to solve the math problems, the teacher wrote them down wrong and Rob ended up practically flunking the test. The results of the accommodation for the exam were so bad that Rob never again asked for extra help throughout the remainder of his undergraduate and postgraduate education.

On June 15, 1997, Rob graduated from Algonquin and received his high school diploma. His graduating class gave him a standing ovation and a cash gift, as well.

Rob's High School graduation

Since Mark was a professor at Bentley University, Rob was

allowed to take classes on a part-time basis. He had learned to drive and had his own wheelchair-accessible van. His classes were at different times than Reed's, so they didn't drive in to Bentley together. Although someone went with him at first, Rob drove himself to school and took his own notes. He used a writing bird to help him write for the first couple of years after the accident. He'd wrap his hand around the bird and then his arm moved the bird around to write for him. Later Rob figured out how to thread a pencil between his fingers to hold on to it, and then he used his arm to make the pencil write. Not having to use the writing bird made writing much easier.

CHAPTER 25

FOUR MONTHS HAD gone by and it was finally time for Reed's tracheal reduction surgery at Mass General Hospital. The surgery began at 8:00 a.m. and continued until noon that day. The doctor told me that the procedure went very well, "just as expected." Three centimeters (about 1 ¼ inch) of Reed's trachea were removed and both healthy ends were stitched together. Then a new opening in Reed's throat was put about one centimeter below the original site. I was told that it was a very tight fit, so hopefully we wouldn't have to deal with the severe air leak any longer. Reed's chin was sewn to his chest with some three-inch long stitches so that he wouldn't accidentally move his head, extend his neck, and tear the trachea apart where it had been sewn together. Then he was moved into the intensive care unit (ICU) for twenty-four hours, so I went home to get some sleep.

Reed was in Mass General for two weeks. One evening his sister Raelene, who was home for the summer, visited him and brought a movie for them both to watch. In the middle of the movie a nurse came in and casually asked, "What movie are you watching?"

Raelene answered, "*Cutthroat Island.*" The nurse got a terrible look on her face and left the room, probably thinking Raelene had a sick sense of humor. But Raelene hadn't thought about Reed's "cut throat" when she rented the newly released movie. She just thought Reed would enjoy the action-packed adventure. She and Reed had a good laugh over it.

With the surgery done and Reed's recovery going well we were hoping things would settle into a calmer routine, but life didn't work that way for us.

Even though it had been two years since the accident, our community continued to support us. The third annual run/walk for Reed and Rob was held in June 1997, and there were six hundred participants. After the race our family provided a barbecue at the park. We were all enjoying ourselves when someone yelled that Natalie was hurt. She had been swinging really high on one of the swings and was about ten feet off the ground when the seat snapped, sending her straight down to the ground. She landed on her back, neck, and head, and lay there in terrible pain.

We took her to the doctor and learned that luckily she hadn't broken any bones. She wore a cervical collar for over a week, though, and then began physical therapy. Natalie was so unhappy that she had to miss girls' camp with the young women of our church congregation. Backpacking and sleeping on the ground were definitely not going to work for her. She had also been looking forward to a trip to New York with Kent and a bunch of youth and adults from church, which she also had to miss. Instead of trying to travel, Natalie decided to rest and get the therapy she needed so she could enjoy the rest of her summer.

In July, Reed and Rob went to the Framingham Union Hospital to get their wisdom teeth out. They checked into the hospital the evening before the surgery so that the doctor could get an early start. The next morning I was in the operating room with Reed just in case the doctor needed my help with adjusting his ventilator or moving his chair while he was under anesthesia. Reed's four wisdom teeth came out without breaking, but Rob wasn't quite so fortunate. His teeth had to be drilled into pieces to get them out because the roots were curved outwards like fish hooks.

I was in the recovery room with Reed and Rob when I got a phone call from the New Hampshire Boy Scout Camp where Kent had gone for the week. I was told that Kent had taken a hockey-ball shot to his eye and was in the hospital, so he needed someone to come and pick him up.

There I sat in the hospital with two of my sons recovering from oral surgery, and now my third son was in a hospital in a completely different state!

I called Mark at work and told him what had happened. Our original plan was for Mark to pick Rob up from the hospital after work that day and take him home. I was going to stay overnight at the hospital with Reed, since his physical condition was more critical than Rob's and the doctor wanted to observe him an additional night. We changed our schedules so that I stayed with Reed and Rob (the hospital decided to keep Rob another night, too), and Mark drove to New Hampshire to bring Kent home.

At the hospital in New Hampshire the doctor told Mark that Kent could go home, but that he would have to lie still for several days while his eye healed. Kent had been looking forward to going to the Boy Scouts of America National Jamboree in Virginia two weeks later, and he was worried that he wouldn't be able to go. When the doctor told him that if he was very careful for the next two weeks he might still be able to attend, he was really relieved.

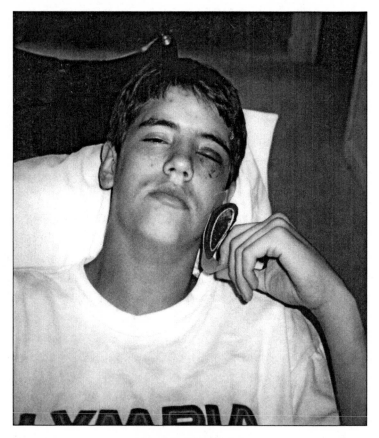

1997 Kent's eye injury

The next day I brought Reed and Rob home and saw Kent's eye. It was swollen and badly bruised, so he fit right in with Reed and Rob, who were also swollen and bruised from their oral surgeries. In fact, Rob's surgery was so difficult that he was bruised all the way down to his chest.

1997 Reed after oral surgery

1997 Rob after oral surgery

I had planned on Kent's and Mark's help with Reed and Rob, so with Natalie's neck somewhat better we had let her go to Martha's Vineyard with her friend's family. Our live-in PCA had gone home to visit her family for the week, as well, so we didn't have any extra help at home. Then, to top it off, our nurse called and told us that there had been a death in her family, so she wouldn't be in until the following week.

We could have used all of that help, but Mark was home, so I figured the two of us could handle it. The next morning, however, Mark went outside to trim some bushes. When he bent over to get to some plants under the boys' ramp, he threw his back out. He couldn't move at all, not even to get out from under the ramp. Kent and I took Rob's wheelchair out and loaded Mark into it to get him into the house. So much for having Mark's help taking care of everyone else.

I spent the weekend at home with my four men all laid up with various disabilities. I took care of Reed and Rob day and night, including turning them in the middle of the night. Mark and Kent needed care, too. I was exhausted. Now, Mark knew that when I was tired he'd better not tease me because it just made me mad, but when Reed and Rob were the ones who started it, Mark joined in with the other three guys in teasing me.

Reed needed some medication and called out, "Mom!"

Then right after that Rob wanted some breakfast so he called, "Mom!"

Mark decided it was a funny joke and yelled from the couch, "Sheryl!"

And Kent, not needing anything, but not wanting to be left out said, "Mom!"

At first I was really frustrated. Then I realized they were all teasing, so I laughed. "This is so unbelievable! Here I have four strong men in the house, and not one of you can help me!"

It was important that we maintain a sense of humor, since it was either laugh or cry.

I wake up late, gotta get the kids to school,
Racin' to work, breakin' every traffic rule.
I don't have time to do the things I should.
I never expected this was motherhood.

'Cause I work all day, don't have time for play,
And I know I'm getting' older 'cause my hair is turnin' gray
From fightin' dragons all day.
I'm fightin' dragons all day.

Sheryl Nixon, 1986

four strong men in the house, and not one of you can help me!"

It was important that we maintain a sense of humor, since it was either laugh or cry.

I wake up late, gotta get the kids to school,
Racin' to work, breakin' every traffic rule.
I don't have time to do the things I should.
I never expected this was motherhood.

'Cause I work all day, don't have time for play,
And I know I'm getting' older 'cause my hair is turnin' gray
From fightin' dragons all day.
I'm fightin' dragons all day.

Sheryl Nixon, 1986

CHAPTER **26**

ROB AND I were at a doctor's appointment when we learned about a five-week intensive therapy camp for the disabled called Shake-A-Leg. The camp was held in Newport, Rhode Island, about 1 ½ hours from our home, so we decided to check it out. Shake-A-Leg provided caregivers to help their clients with any personal needs, so Rob could actually stay there for the full five weeks and receive therapy to help him learn how to become more independent. Mark and I were pretty nervous about leaving him there for so long, but realizing that he could really benefit from the program, Rob wanted to give it a try. We signed him up to begin the program that summer. Reed was unable to attend the camp because he was on a ventilator and his injury was much too severe to have the caretakers there try to help him.

Mark and Raelene drove Rob to Shake-A-Leg on June 21, 1998. There were several challenges Rob had to deal with at the beginning of the therapy program. He had been used to sleeping in a hospital bed at home, which allowed him to raise and lower the bed for transfers in and out of his wheelchair. It was difficult for him when he had only a regular twin bed at Shake-A-Leg. To get from the chair to the bed, Rob used a slide board to put between the chair and the bed. Then he gradually scooted himself over the board until he was on the bed. If the bed was higher or lower than his chair, the board wouldn't go straight across, and his transfers would be that much more difficult.

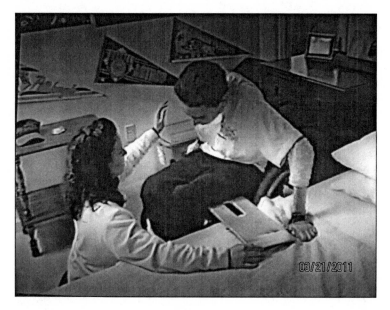

Slide board

Since Rob didn't have the use of his stomach muscles, he couldn't just sit up in bed like an able-bodied person. At home he had used a trapeze or metal triangle hooked above his bed to loop his arm through and pull himself up into a sitting position. But Shake-A-Leg didn't have a trapeze, either. Rob quickly adjusted to these challenges and became stronger in the process.

During the five-week camp, Rob thrived. He went snorkeling, sailing, kayaking, hand biking, and even parasailing!

He came home with a "can do" attitude, preferring to think of all the things he could do instead of the things he couldn't. At Shake-A-Leg Rob learned to transfer from his chair to his bed or vice versa without the use of a slide board. Without a trapeze to help himself sit up, Rob figured out that if he sat on his hands or put his hands in his pockets, he could use his shoulder muscles to wiggle himself up into a sitting position, a feat no one at Shake-A-Leg had ever thought of before. Even Rob's doctors and physical therapists at home were impressed.

Rob parasailing

Rob also learned how to feed himself without the use of a special device to hold the fork or spoon for him. Similar to the way he held a pencil or pen, he threaded the utensil through his fingers to hold it and his arm did the rest. Rob learned that he could do far more for himself than he'd thought possible before Shake-A-Leg.

From that point on there was no stopping him. He tried everything. There were some things that he obviously couldn't do, like walk, but he found there were many things he could do that he would never have tried before his experience at Shake-A-Leg.

Rob's roommate was a paraplegic (paralyzed from the

waist down), so he had the use of his arms and hands, as well as upper body strength. The young man was unhappy with his situation and wasn't trying very hard, so Rob seemed to have nearly as much function as his roommate. Out of all the patients at Shake-A-Leg that summer, Rob's spinal cord injury was the worst, but because he tried every activity available, everyone called him "super-quad."

Rob learned to do a lot more than anyone expected. As time went on his roommate saw everything Rob was doing and began to realize how much he was able to do for himself, and he finally began making some progress.

⟩⟩⟩↙

When Rob got home, our family packed up and flew out west to attend several family reunions. One of the reunions was in Utah. The first day was spent at Seven Peaks, a water park with some pretty incredible water slides. Jeff and Mark, Rob's brothers-in-law, convinced him to go down one of the big slides with them. They carried him to the top of the slide, and then Rob went down on a tube by himself. We were all pretty amazed and impressed at the time, but now looking back on the event, Rob says he would never do it again. It really was too dangerous with his limited physical abilities.

Reed, of course, couldn't do anything at the water park. It was way too hot to just sit outside, so he and I went shopping at a nearby mall. Shopping quickly became Reed's and my entertainment whenever there was an activity that he couldn't participate in. As a result of our shopping over the years of vacations and other trips, Reed has several collections that he still works on: seashells, Olympic and sports pins, rocks and minerals, and sports memorabilia. His collections are pretty impressive.

For the next family reunion that summer, we took a three-car caravan and drove from Salt Lake City, Utah, to Idaho Falls, Idaho. I brought up the rear of the caravan driving the rented van with Reed, Rob, and Kent. About an hour outside of Salt Lake City I ran over something that looked like a fireman's hose: cloth with a metal end. The speed limit was seventy-five miles per hour and the four lanes of traffic were really moving along, so I didn't see the object until after the car in front of me (Mark and Natalie) ran over it. Then I had only a second or two to react, which wasn't enough time. I heard a loud "clank," and I was really worried that the oil pan had been punctured. I watched the oil pressure gauge closely as we continued traveling, but the gauge stayed the same throughout the whole road trip, so I eventually forgot about it.

Three hours later we pulled into the motel in Idaho Falls, parked our cars, and got out to visit with the other relatives who were arriving. It was then that I noticed we had a flat rear tire on the driver's side of the van, right where I had heard the "clank" several hours earlier. I looked closely and saw a big hole in the sidewall of the tire, a very unusual place. I blinked as I realized that a miracle had taken place. The only way that hole could have gotten there was from the object I'd run over hours before, but the Lord had kept the tire inflated until we had reached our destination safe and sound. Then the tire went flat. If we'd had a flat tire when we first ran over the object with the heavy traffic and the speed we were going, we would certainly have all been killed in a crash. And who knows how many others would have been involved. I knew that our lives had been preserved for some unknown purpose.

There was a heat wave that summer in Idaho, so even though we kept Reed in the shade for the outdoor activities, his temperature quickly got up to 102.4 degrees. The only place to cool him down was in the van with the air condition-ing blowing on him full blast, so that's where Reed and I spent the rest of the day.

Even after several hours in a cool van, Reed's temperature was still over one hundred degrees. One of the results of the accident and Reed's SCI was that his internal thermostat was broken. If the temperature was hot outside, Reed's tempera-ture went up, but if it was cold, his temperature went way down. Either way, it would take us most of the day to regu-late him. We always had to monitor Reed's temperature very closely, and we still do.

After Shake-A-Leg Rob continued to get more indepen-dent and was eventually able to handle all of his personal needs: bowel care, showering, and dressing. I remember the first time I saw Rob trying to put a sock on his foot. Without the use of his hands and fingers, and no stomach muscles to help, the process was painstakingly slow. In fact, when Mark watched Rob put his sock on the first time, it was so heart-breaking that he had to leave the room. Rob used his wrists to gradually scoot the sock on and it took him a good forty-five minutes to do it. Now he can get dressed and in his chair in less time than it took earlier for just one sock.

Our third reunion that summer was a Packard (my mom's maiden name) family reunion in Colorado. We had an experi-ence there that showed us just how much Rob had progressed. One of my cousins-in-law at the reunion was a neurologist. He was fascinated with Reed and Rob and told Mark that Rob looked like he was a C7 injury level. Mark told him that Rob was a level C5/6, but my cousin-in-law doubted that. A little later, after doing his own evaluation on Rob, my cousin-in-law found Mark and said, "You're right! Rob *is* a C5/6! I'm very surprised. He has much more function than I would have expected with that level of injury. It's not the first time I've seen more function with a C5/6 injury level, but it is very rare. This is a good representation of how hard Rob worked during his physical therapy."

Mark knew Rob was a C5/6 all along, but it was really interesting that Rob had learned how to do so much that he'd fooled even a neurologist!

Another time, Rob was at the hospital being evaluated for a new wheelchair. Rob showed the physical therapist what he could do and the function he had. The therapist was shocked and called all of the other therapists in to watch Rob do things that he technically shouldn't have been able to do so they could teach their patients how to function better. Rob was pleased that in helping himself he was able to help other quadriplegics in their rehabilitation, too.

At home one day, Rob was trying to put a CD in his CD player when it dropped on the floor. I asked him if he wanted me to pick it up for him and he said no, he was going to try to pick it up himself. Rob spent the next fifteen minutes trying different ways to pick up that CD. He couldn't use two hands because it was too far down to reach, and if he stretched with both arms he'd fall out of his chair. So while hanging onto his chair with one arm he was finally able to pick up the CD by putting his pinkie finger in the hole of the CD and slowly wiggling it until the CD hooked onto his finger.

It was so hard for me to stand there and watch as he struggled time and again. I would have gladly picked up the CD for him. I had to stop myself and allow him the time necessary to learn on his own. It was a good thing he was self-motivated and determined to do things for himself, because if he hadn't been, I'm sure I would have done too much for him and he wouldn't have progressed nearly as far or as fast. Rob continued to impress us by earning his Eagle Scout award that year.

Now that Rob was more independent, he began preparing to serve a mission for The Church of Jesus Christ of Latter-day Saints. He started studying every available minute. With Rob's level of disability, Mark and I didn't think he would physically be able to serve a mission. It came as a total surprise to us when he showed us his completed mission application papers. In mid-September Rob received news that he was called to the Massachusetts, Boston Mission and he would begin serving in October. That gave us only two weeks to make the necessary preparations.

It was a common practice to have prospective missionaries and their families speak and/or sing at church the Sunday before beginning their missions (referred to as a missionary farewell). Many times an open house was held afterwards so that everyone could congratulate the missionary. We were very busy getting everything ready for the farewell, the open house, and the mission itself.

With such a short amount of time before Rob's farewell, it never occurred to me to write a song to sing, because I was still trying to finish the song I'd started years before and hadn't made any progress. Besides, I had focused all my efforts on the open house, which would be held at our home. Then I woke up at 1:30 one morning with thoughts about a song for Rob's farewell. In my mind I said, "Wait a minute and let me grab a pencil and paper." And that was just about how fast the song came to me. By 3:30 that morning, I'd written down all of the words and I went back to bed. Over the next couple of days I wrote the music while I sincerely thanked the Lord for sending me such a beautiful and powerful song. The spiritual connection I felt through my music was beginning to return.

Rob going on mission

At Rob's farewell I sang my new song, "I Know God Lives."

I remember scriptures that my mother read to me
Like Moses and the Israelites and how God set them free.
She also told me of a man whose life was free from sin.
Then she shared the testimony she had gained of Him.

I know God lives. I know His plan.
I know through Jesus Christ, Father's work began.
I know He lived and died for me,

So I could be with Him eternally.

Through the coming years, I get to teach about His word.
I'll try to share His love, and I will do my best to serve.
I'll search for those who seek for Jesus Christ, to find His way,
Teach His gospel truths, and be a witness for His name.

My faith in God has strengthened; I've found power in His word,
And now the time has come for me to go and serve the Lord.
All my life I've waited, waited for this day,
Waited for the time when I could stand alone and say,

"I know God lives! I know His plan!
I know through Jesus Christ, Father's work began!
I know He lived and died for me,
So I could be with Him eternally."

I know He lives, and He loves me.
I want to be with Him eternally.

I Know God Lives, Sheryl Nixon, 1999

After my song it was Rob's turn to speak. He said, "Over the past several years people have served me, and now I am finally able to serve others." Reed gave a beautiful closing prayer asking God to "help Rob be able to maximize all of the progress he has made to this point."

Rob was kept busy with the media after the meeting and at our home during the open house. We had over two hundred people in and out that evening, since so many neighbors, friends, and church members came to congratulate Rob and to share their best wishes. Everything about the whole day was unbelievably uplifting.

The plan for Rob's living arrangements on his mission was to live at home and drive his van into Boston each day to serve in the mission office. Rob wondered if he would ever be allowed to live in a mission apartment and proselyte door to door with another missionary as his companion. What a surprise it was when Rob was on his way driving to the mission office to report for his first day as a missionary and I got a phone call from his Mission President, Dale Murphy (baseball's two-time National League Most Valuable Player for the Atlanta Braves). President Murphy asked me if it would be possible to have Rob with a missionary companion, staying there in Boston in an apartment within two days. Wow, was I surprised!

With Rob not living at home where I could keep his laundry caught up, I had to buy him more clothes. That way he would have enough to last him through the week until his preparation day (usually on a Monday when missionaries did their grocery shopping, laundry, letter writing, etc.) when he could do his own laundry. Rob was very happy to be living like any other missionary. There were many challenges, but he was willing to find solutions for them.

In one of Rob's apartments there were a couple of stairs into the kitchen and bathroom. After trying to make it work but not finding any success, Rob was transferred to a different apartment. His mission companions were very helpful if he needed anything, even carrying him up the stairs when they were visiting someone on a second or third floor with no elevator in the building.

Every now and then Rob had a doctor's appointment to

have his Baclofen pump refilled, so once in a while he and his missionary companion stopped by our house to pick up medical supplies he was short on. Once, there wasn't enough time for them to make it back to their apartment before their curfew, so they got permission to spend the night at home. Rob's van was parked behind Reed's van, so the next morning when Reed was ready to leave for school, I had to move Rob's van.

As soon as I got in the van I could smell a horrible odor, like an electrical burning smell. I took the van right down to the repair shop and found out that it needed to be towed to the dealership. Apparently, during the night Rob's van had caught fire and burned a lot of the wiring under the floor. The carpet had actually melted to the floor of the van! Mark and I were very thankful that circumstances had prevented Rob and his missionary companion from driving the two hours back to their apartment the night before.

While Rob's van got repaired, he and his companion used a mission car. Rob wasn't very happy to be without his van because he couldn't drive the mission car, and his companion had to lift him in and out of the car anytime they went somewhere. It was a good thing Rob was skinny, because it was six weeks of lifting for his companion before his van came back from the dealership.

At first Rob was called on a one-year mission, but when the year was nearly over he asked President Murphy if he could extend for another year. He really wanted to serve a full-time, two-year mission like any other missionary would do. President Murphy looked into it and approved the extension.

When Rob was about halfway through the second year of his mission, his Baclofen pump had to be replaced. At that point in time the pumps had a life of three to five years, but now they last more like five to seven years. Rob came home for two weeks to have the procedure done and time to recover. He wasn't quite up to par when he returned to his mission and could probably have used another week to recover, but he was eager to get back to his missionary work.

Rob faithfully wrote us a letter every week and we loved hearing about his mission experiences. My favorite letter was the one where he told us about his first baptism. The LDS church baptizes by immersion, so Rob had to be in the water. Since his wheelchair wasn't supposed to be in the water, his mission companion got Rob's shower bench and Rob sat on it to keep it from floating. That would have worked great, except Rob's legs floated! Rob suspected that might happen, so he had brought along some ankle weights. After someone got the weights around his ankles to keep his legs from floating, Rob knew that he didn't have enough upper body strength to hold himself in a sitting position in the water, so he asked another missionary to stand behind him in the water to hold him upright.

When people are baptized by immersion, they are lowered down into the water by the person baptizing them and then immediately brought back up out of the water. Well, Rob could get the woman down into the water, but he didn't have enough balance or strength in his arms to bring her back up. The poor girl could have drowned! To prevent this, Rob asked one more missionary to stand by him to help lift the lady up out of the water. The baptism went perfectly, but the joke around the mission was, "How many missionaries does it take to baptize a young woman? Three, of course!"

After reading Rob's letter about the baptism, I knew that for him the sky was the limit!

CHAPTER **27**

REED'S LUNG DOCTOR (Pulmonologist) frequently looked into various methods of keeping his lungs healthy and improving his quality of life. The first device she had Reed try was called a Passe Muir valve. It worked similar to a one-way valve, allowing Reed to control the exhale with his mouth and nose instead of the air escaping through his trachea tube. The process allowed him to speak almost continuously if he wanted.

Reed didn't like the valve at first because it made his chest sore and dried out his lungs. He began getting nebulizer treatments of saline (salt water) to help humidify his lungs and the treatments helped a lot. Over time Reed developed a tolerance to the changes in his lungs and enjoyed the ability he had to speak in complete sentences. The Passe Muir valve gave Reed more confidence to speak and answer questions in his college classes. He was finally able to carry on a normal conversation, too!

During Reed's pulmonologist's research, she also found information about an in-exsufflator or "cough machine," which basically simulated a cough. Since Reed couldn't cough by himself to remove mucus from his lungs (because he didn't have the use of his chest and abdominal muscles), he frequently got pneumonia. Once he began using the in-exsufflator his bouts with pneumonia dramatically decreased. The machine worked by giving Reed a breath and then sucking out more air than went in, to simulate a cough and pull the mucus out of his lungs. We used the machine several times every day and Reed became much healthier as a result.

Another procedure Reed's pulmonologist researched was inserting a diaphragm pacemaker. Before the procedure could be done though, a test had to be performed on Reed's phrenic nerves, located on both sides of his neck. These nerves, originating at the third, fourth, and fifth cervical vertebrae, stimulated the diaphragm to contract, which resulted in a breath. The test would be performed at the Yale Medical Center in New Haven, Connecticut, and would determine whether or not Reed was a candidate for the procedure of putting a pacemaker on his diaphragm so he could breathe on his own. He would have to be in the hospital for a week for the test.

I had such high hopes for Reed. I just knew that qualifying for the procedure would be an incredible opportunity to improve his quality of life. The biggest change would be in Reed's having more privacy and independence. He wouldn't always require having someone with him, or at least within hearing distance. Solitude can sometimes be a quiet, wonderful, and calming experience.

Without the ventilator, our family would also have much more flexibility. We wouldn't have to hurry home when a nurse's shift was over; Reed could just wait a little while until we got there. And help would be much more readily available because we wouldn't have to train someone in trachea care and how to work the ventilator before they could be alone with Reed.

We decided to schedule the test during Bentley's spring break. By going that particular week, Reed wouldn't miss any school. He and I drove the two hours to the New Haven Hospital in Connecticut. I had a lot of time to ponder and pray during that week with Reed. I couldn't think of one reason why the procedure wouldn't be a tremendous blessing for him. In my prayers I expressed my faith and trust in God and told myself that if it was His will, Reed would be a good candidate for the surgery, and if Reed wasn't, then the Lord had something else in mind.

Although I thought I had complete faith and trust in God, I guess I really didn't, because I was devastated when I was told that there was no response from either of Reed's phrenic nerves. I stood in the corner of his room while the doctors and nurses put the test equipment away and I wept. Why wasn't there ever good news for Reed?

♪♪♪♪

Back at home, during one of Reed's hospital stays when Mark was visiting, he noticed a pressure sore on Reed's tailbone. When Mark got home that evening, he told me about the sore (too much pressure in one place will eventually cause the skin to break down); we both knew that we needed to keep an eye on it. Mark was at the hospital the next night and told the nurse that the pressure sore needed to be watched very closely.

When Reed got home from the hospital, we made sure the home nurses knew about the sore, too, so they could do what was necessary to heal it. The Visiting Nurses Association (VNA) sent a wound nurse to our house to evaluate the skin breakdown. She put some cream on the pressure sore and covered it with a special bandage that was supposed to help in the healing process. The problem was that we didn't know what was causing the sore in the first place, and unless we could find the cause and eliminate it, we probably couldn't keep the pressure sore from getting worse.

I tried and tried to figure out what was causing the skin breakdown. It looked like a long rectangle about ½ inch x 2 inches, so at first, I thought maybe the zipper on Reed's seat cushion cover was causing the problem. I rotated the cushion 180 degrees, but nothing changed and the sore got worse. After an entire year of trying to heal the wound, I took Reed to a dermatologist hoping for some answers. The doctor took a culture and put Reed on an antibiotic for ten days. She also tried several different creams and medicines, but without knowing what was causing the wound in the first place, we didn't make much progress.

Finally, two years after Mark first saw the pressure sore on Reed's bottom, I found the cause of the skin breakdown. The flat metal platform where the cushion sat on Reed's wheelchair wasn't actually flat. The metal curved down about ½ inch at the front under Reed's knees and curved up a ½ inch at the back, under the back rest of the chair. I hadn't felt that metal lip before because it was further back than I had looked. When I finally felt that lip I knew it was what was causing Reed's wound. What irony! Reed's wheelchair, which was supposed to benefit him, ended up causing a serious wound. It was evident to me that the designers of the wheelchair were *not* paralyzed, and they'd made a horrible error in their design.

During the day, as Reed sat in his wheelchair, his seat cushion gradually slid a little bit forward and Reed slid down with it. As a result, instead of sitting on the cushion the last half of the day, he sat right on that metal lip. After sitting on the metal day after day, the pressure sore became a wound. I immediately turned that metal slab upside down so that the back curved down and the front curved up. The metal that curved up never touched the backs of Reed's knees, so it was a perfect solution.

Eventually, we learned that there was a wound clinic in the plastic surgery department of UMASS. We were very upset that the VNA wound nurse hadn't told us that such a place existed. Because Reed's pressure sore had turned into a big wound, I made an appointment that very day.

The plastic surgeon gradually scraped the dead tissue out of the ulcer on Reed's bottom until after many appointments we finally saw the full extent of the damage that had been done. The hole was so deep it went all the way to the bone, and the wound was big enough that I could have put a large egg in it. I felt terrible that it had taken me so long to figure out what was causing the pressure and that I couldn't find anyone to help me solve the problem.

❧❧❧

One of the many times Reed was in the hospital was for blood pressure instability. One minute it was high, and then the next time it was checked it was so low that it didn't even register on the monitor. He also had a constant bad stomachache. Eventually Reed was diagnosed with atypical pneumonia, which doesn't show up on x-rays, and a stomachache is often a symptom. He was put on antibiotics to clear it up.

After checking the ulcer on Reed's behind, his doctor began wondering if the wound was causing some of Reed's other health problems, so he called in Reed's plastic surgeon to ask him what he thought. When the plastic surgeon got to Reed's room he had the representative of a wound-healing machine company with him. The representative told us about his product and we decided to give it a try. The machine included a type of sponge that was put into Reed's wound and taped down tight so it would make an airtight suction. Then the machine was hooked up to the sponge.

As the machine ran it gently increased the blood flow to the wound. Since blood is what promotes healing by bringing oxygen, fluids, and nutrition to the area, the system worked really well and fairly soon we saw some improvement. Originally, Reed's plastic surgeon had planned to get the wound to heal to a certain point and, not expecting it to close entirely on its own, he would take a patch or flap of skin from Reed's bottom and stitch it over the wound and then let everything heal. He didn't want to use the flap if he didn't have to, though, because that particular procedure could be performed only a few times over Reed's entire life, and Reed was still very young.

The suction machine for Reed's wound was literally a "pain in the butt"! If the system hadn't worked so well we never would have continued using it. It was really hard to keep that suction going. If there was a leak at all it would sound an alarm. Sometimes, just after we had finally gotten Reed dressed and in his chair, the alarm would go off. Then we would have to get him back in bed and start all over again with the tape. If the alarm ever went off at school, we just had to leave class and come home.

There finally came a point where the wound seemed to reach a plateau, so we stopped using the machine. By then Reed's plastic surgeon had come up with another solution. He put a dry type of material into the wound, which was supposed to pull the blood flow toward the damaged area. Although the material went in dry, as it soaked up fluids it became a gel. The wound began to heal again and Reed's doctors were amazed at the quick progress. As time went on and the wound got smaller, less and less of the material had to be put into the hole, until it finally closed up completely! Reed didn't have to go through another surgery after all!

Christopher Reeve passed away due to skin breakdown or pressure sores. The sores became so badly infected that they caused his whole body to become septic (full of bacteria) which eventually resulted in heart failure. Now Mark and I look back on Reed's pressure sore and realize that Reed was incredibly blessed that his wound never once got infected, especially since it was located in a place where germs are common. We continued to be amazed that the wound closed up completely on its own. We considered the healing a great blessing.

❧❧❧

One Sunday morning I was getting ready to put dinner in the oven while Mark was in with Reed getting him ready for church, when suddenly Mark yelled, "Sheryl!"

I ran into Reed's room and found Reed unconscious and turning gray with Mark bagging him as fast as he could. "Do you want me to call 911?" I asked, but Mark thought he could get Reed to respond after bagging him a little longer. Almost thirty seconds later I was nearing the panic stage when Reed finally started getting color back in his face. Mark and I breathed a huge sigh of relief. That was too scary!

Apparently, Mark had been shaving Reed and had disconnected his trachea tube for a couple of breaths, which he had done many times without a problem. This time though, Reed had passed out. After church when I told our live-in PCA what had happened that morning, he remembered that a similar, but much shorter and less traumatic experience had happened a couple of nights before, but he had forgotten to tell us about it when he woke up the next afternoon.

Monday morning I called the doctor and told her what had happened over the weekend. She thought we should have taken Reed to the hospital, but from past experience we knew that nothing would have happened at the hospital over the weekend. Any testing was almost always put off until Monday anyway, so we had decided to wait. The doctor told me to take Reed to the ER.

The home nurse and I got Reed dressed, in his chair, and loaded up into the van, but at UMASS we ended up sitting in the waiting room for over three and a half hours. I kept asking, "How much longer?"

Over and over I was told, "As soon as we have a spot for him in the ER, we'll get him in." The hospital was always full, and I don't think there was ever a time we didn't have to wait several hours for a room.

Because hospitals are generally kept on the cool side, I began to worry about Reed's temperature. At first it went down gradually, but then it dropped faster and faster as time went on. When Reed's temperature got to 96.2, my patience was gone. In those few hours at the hospital Reed was getting worse. I told the front desk I couldn't wait any longer and was taking him home. The nurse urged us to wait longer— that Reed would be seen in a short while—but enough was enough! We left.

However, while Reed and I were at the hospital, we had both noticed that if a sick or injured person arrived in an ambulance they were taken directly back to the ER. We decided that from then on we would always have Reed transported to the hospital in an ambulance. As a result, we never again had to wait for hours just to get *into* the ER, let alone wait for a room.

The next day Reed's doctor called and asked me why he wasn't seen by an ER physician. After I explained, she asked me to bring Reed to her office at the hospital. We found out that Reed had pneumonia and a collapsed lung. The doctor gave him a broncoscopy (a procedure where the doctor goes down through Reed's trachea tube with a small light, camera, and suction instrument to inspect the tissue) to clear the mucus out of his lung, but even then the lung only partially inflated. Reed was put on two antibiotics to clear up the pneumonia, and Gentamicin for his collapsed lung. Gentamicin is a very strong antibiotic and is given only through an IV or an injection.

The next morning while Reed was in the shower, he felt a strange, numb, tingling sensation on his left side. When the same thing happened two days later, the doctor replaced the Gentamicin with another medicine, Tobramycin, which still had to be given through an IV or shot.

We had been planning a vacation to Pennsylvania for months and were supposed to leave that weekend, so we didn't want Reed to be on an IV. The doctor said that Reed could go on the trip with us if I would give him the Tobramycin shots three times a day. Yuck! I had never given a shot before and I really didn't want to. I didn't sign up to be a nurse for Reed; I just wanted to be his mother. I thought, "When will my medical education ever end?"

Oh well, if that's what had to be done, I would do it. The day before we left on our vacation we were relieved to learn that Reed's lung had re-inflated. I still had to give him the shots three times a day, but I managed. The Tobramycin worked much better and Reed didn't experience any negative side effects. The trip to Pennsylvania was one of Reed's all-time favorite vacations.

CHAPTER **28**

ROB COMPLETED HIS two-year mission for the Church in the fall of 2000. He and Reed both attended Bentley University in January 2001, but Rob planned to transfer to Brigham Young University (BYU) in the fall. Mark told Rob that he should at least take one accounting class before leaving, since Bentley was a business university and accounting was one of its specialties. Besides, Mark taught accounting and could help a little if Rob had any questions.

Rob didn't know what he was going to major in, so he took the accounting class. It wasn't Mark's class, but Rob really enjoyed it. He decided to major in accounting at BYU, which had one of the top accounting programs in the country. Rob wasn't sure he would go into accounting as a profession, but he knew that having an accounting background would help in whatever he chose to do for a living.

In June of that year, I went to Utah for my thirtieth high school class reunion. While I was there I decided to check on Rob's housing for the fall semester. I was frustrated when I couldn't find a single off-campus apartment with a roll-in shower. I finally ended up checking the dorms on-campus and found a good-sized private room that had a roll-in shower. I told the manager that I'd be back to take the room after I got Rob registered for the fall semester.

But when I went to register Rob, I found out that he could stay in the dorms only if he was a student attending BYU, and it turned out that he was twenty-five credits short of the amount required as a transfer student. As a result, I couldn't get him registered. I learned, however, that the rules for housing were different for night students, so I decided to try registering Rob for night classes. I called Mark and had him fax Rob's Bentley transcript to me. But when I went to register Rob again, I was told that a fax was not adequate; I had to have the original transcript.

I spoke to a counselor in the admissions department, gave him the copy of the transcript, and explained my problem. My flight back to Boston was the following day, and I really needed to have Rob's school and housing settled before I went home. I told the counselor that Rob had just finished his finals at Bentley University and had gotten A's for both of his summer courses. Rob also had a 3.94 GPA for the year and a half he had attended Bentley. The counselor took all of the information and asked me to wait while he tried to see what he could do to help.

After a while the counselor returned and asked me, "Do you want the bad news first or the good news?"

I blinked, paused, and then quietly answered, "The bad news."

He replied, "There is no bad news, only good news!" Rob could take night classes during the fall semester until he completed the twenty-five credits he needed. Then he could register as a full-time day student. I hurried back to the housing director to let him know I wanted the room, signed the papers, and paid for the semester.

Kent graduated from high school and attended BYU as well. Rob and Kent lived only two buildings away from each other, so Kent became Rob's PCA that year. They really developed a close relationship as they spent hours together sharing, studying, playing, and simply enjoying life.

Kent received his mission call from the Church to spend two years in the Utah, Provo Mission. Kent was attending BYU at the time he received the call, so he was already there! Rob and Kent finished their semester at BYU in May and came home. Our Northborough church congregation held a missionary farewell for Kent on Sunday, May 26, 2002.

To start the program off, I sang one of my songs.

...When my neighbor passes me....
I'll be a good example of the things I know are true.

And be an instrument in Thy hand, serving my fellowman,
Spreading the gospel plan my whole life through.
A humble instrument in Thy hand, serving the best I can...

When I help someone in need, I'll do it with a smile,
Give the best I've got to give, and go the second mile.
Through service love and friendship, I've found that there's a key.
By my serving others, I am really serving Thee....

From, Serving the Best I Can, Sheryl Nixon, 1989

After my song, Reed spoke. He told of an experience he'd had one night when his trachea tube had popped off, so he wasn't breathing. With his ventilator alarm sounding, Reed prayed that his dad would come quickly to reattach the tube. Reed said that he realized that night that he needed to pray more often. He told Kent, "Although you will not face challenges such as not breathing, you will face challenges nonetheless. Prayer will help you through those challenges."

With Kent on a mission, Rob rented a condominium, had the bathroom remodeled to allow a roll-in shower, and moved in. A couple of Rob's cousins, John and Michael Nixon, were attending BYU at the same time and lived close by. Over the next two years each of them worked for Rob as his PCA. Not only did they already have a close relationship, but Rob felt comfortable with them helping him with his personal care. They shared a lot of good times together and made up for some of the difficulties Rob had living with roommates for the first time.

Rob's first roommates were not a good fit for him. Between their personal hygiene and cleanliness issues, Rob struggled. Neither of the roommates was very social and I had really hoped that they would be able to help Rob socially as well as physically, but they didn't do either. When I found out about it, I was so disappointed I started to cry. Rob was now an adult living a long way from home. However, he was still very vulnerable. I was so conflicted. Truthfully, I have the same emotional conflict today. I doubt I will ever be able to stop worrying about him. I frequently had to remind myself that Rob was in the Lord's hands and that in the end everything would work out.

Natalie lived up the street a couple of blocks from where Rob lived, so if he needed help or had any problems, she could run over and help him. Natalie had a steady boyfriend named Joshua Dayton, and he helped Rob, too.

Natalie and Josh were married on November 20, 2001, just two months after the September 11 terrorist attack in New York City, so when we all flew out to Utah for their wedding we had to allow even more time at the airport because of all the security. Rob loved having Natalie and Josh close by, and they often got together to play games or go to the movies. Over the next several years they really enjoyed the time they spent together.

◄◄◄◄

During Rob's first semester at BYU, a friend of ours had anonymously nominated him to be a torch bearer for the 2002 Olympics. Rob was selected! He was certainly deserving of the honor. I couldn't think of a better example of the Olympic spirit, and I was very pleased that others recognized this as well. The torch was traveling throughout the country and would be in Massachusetts around Christmas time. We got a letter telling us that Rob would be carrying the torch in downtown Boston on December 27, 2001. The night of the twenty-seventh was bitterly cold, but several of our family members were there to support Rob. He and Reed were on the evening news with interviews prior to the event, and footage of Rob carrying the torch. It was a pretty big night.

Reed sat in his wheelchair at the spot where Rob's torch was lit and Rob began his specified route at 6:30 p.m. He looked awesome in his 2002 Olympic torch bearer uniform. He absolutely beamed, grinning with a smile from ear to ear, as he carried the torch. At the end of his route, Rob was able to keep his torch, so we had it mounted along with his picture for a wonderful memory.

Rob carrying torch

CHAPTER **29**

IN AUGUST 2002, we learned that Rob had been accepted into Brigham Young University's Marriott Business School and Accounting Program, and that he'd received the coveted University Scholarship for the fall and winter semesters. In addition, as long as Rob continued to get good grades he could renew the scholarship, so it was a huge financial blessing for him. What a contrast to nearly failing his college entrance exams!

I was in Utah the last week in September helping Raelene with a new baby girl, her fourth child, and had been there only two days when I got a call from Rob. He had blood in his urine and he felt pain when he urinated. He also felt pain in his side and stomach, and he had chills. I told Rob I'd meet him at the Utah Valley Regional Medical Center emergency room. I was very disappointed when the ER doctor took a urine specimen, gave Rob a prescription for Cipro, and sent him home.

I spoke to Rob's granddad, who lived close by, and he thought I should take Rob to a urologist. He gave me the name of his urologist and I made an appointment right away. Three days later I picked Rob up for the appointment. I told the urologist that the ER doctor hadn't done anything more than order a urinalysis and give Rob a prescription. I couldn't understand why the doctor hadn't had the urine cultured to see what bacteria was growing and which medicine would kill that particular bug. He just assumed that Cipro would take care of it. But it hadn't, and Rob's urinary tract infection had gotten worse.

Rob was still having pain so the urologist ordered several tests at the hospital for the following week. I told Rob that I'd be happy to go with him when he had the tests, but he said I didn't need to. He thought I should be with Raelene, her kids, and the new baby since that was why I was in Utah in the first place. I took Rob back to his apartment and returned to Raelene's house.

Rob's first test was a VCUG to test for a neurogenic (paralyzed) bladder and to check his kidneys. The first of two bags of dye was delivered into Rob's bloodstream to fill his bladder. Then x-rays were taken to see if his urine was going where it was supposed to. However, before the first bag of dye was in Rob's bloodstream he got a tremendous headache, his blood pressure was elevated, and he was sweating.

Rob asked the hospital technicians if he was experiencing autonomic dysreflexia, but they didn't know what he was talking about. They should have known that autonomic dysreflexia is a life-threatening complication that can be seen in almost anyone with a spinal cord injury (SCI) above the thoracic level 6 (T6) and can cause a stroke. The symptoms of autonomic dysreflexia are a pounding headache (from high blood pressure), blurred vision, goosebumps, and sweating, to name a few. The technicians should have known this, but they didn't.

Rob rested for a little bit and then the technicians tried the test again. They had the same result, so they stopped and went on to the second test. Rob had been fasting and was exhausted. After the tests were finished, he went back to his apartment to sleep. A short time later he woke up in terrible pain and called me at Raelene's house. He told me what had happened at the hospital that morning and he began to cry. He hurt all over and he said that since having the tests he got an excruciating headache whenever he urinated. Rob almost never complained when he wasn't feeling well. He usually just said, "I'll live," so this time I knew his pain was horrible.

I told Rob I'd call the doctor and call him right back. The urologist said Rob had autonomic dysreflexia and he told me I needed to get him to the ER as soon as possible. The doctor asked me to call him as soon as we got there.

At the hospital a nurse monitored Rob's blood pressure until an ER doctor finally came. I administered percussion and crede on Rob (tapping on his bladder and applying pressure to bring on urination) while the doctor was there, so he could see what happened each time Rob urinated. Rob sat there crying and nearly dying with pain; his blood pressure was up to 166/100. The ER doctor immediately left to call Rob's urologist. When the urologist arrived at the hospital, he said that he could get a Foley (internal) catheter to drain Rob's urine, but that it might make things worse. Although I was supposed to fly home to Boston the next day, I told the doctor that I wasn't going to go home with Rob in so much pain. He said they would keep Rob in the hospital overnight for observation and decide the following day what their course of action would be. As the night progressed, Rob's headache returned every time he urinated, and then it took a long time afterward to alleviate his pain.

The doctor ordered a shot of pain medication to block Rob's nerve receptors and then put a Foley catheter into Rob's bladder. He said that Rob's bladder was spasming so badly that the urine was hardly draining out at all. The shot and catheter seemed to help a little, and pretty soon Rob fell asleep. I hurried back to Raelene's house to grab an overnight bag and finally fell asleep in the reclining chair beside Rob's bed at 1:00 a.m.

The next morning when Rob had his bowel routine the terrific headache returned, and since the Foley catheter had eased the urination headache, we knew there was something else wrong. Rob and I waited for hours to find out what would happen next. Eventually, the urologist came in and told us that he thought Rob needed to be seen by a colleague of his who had more experience with neurological matters. But when he tried to get an appointment with his colleague—or any neurologist, for that matter—no one was available for an entire week!

Rob's urologist finally talked to a doctor who was familiar with very sensitive drugs and he decided to gradually start Rob on Cardizem to lower his blood pressure. However, the drug had to be given in the hospital so that Rob's blood pressure didn't go too low. Rob had to stay in the hospital four more days. I called the airline from the hospital and changed my ticket to an open-ended ticket, which meant I could fly back home whenever I wanted as long as the plane had an available seat.

I was very disappointed with the care Rob received at the hospital during those next four days. It seemed as though no one had ever dealt with a paralyzed patient before! When I asked for anything for Rob, such as a "bed bag" (a bag that hangs by the bedside to collect urine), they didn't know what I was talking about. I was really glad that I decided to stay with Rob so that I could make sure he got the care he needed.

I asked Rob to call his professors at BYU to let them know that he was going to miss classes for the rest of the week, and he did. However, he never mentioned that he was in the hospital! He wanted to be treated like other students and he didn't want to get preferential treatment. But what Rob didn't seem to realize was that any able-bodied student would definitely use a hospital stay as an excuse for special treatment.

Rob was finally released from the hospital that weekend

and I flew home. But after spending ten days with Raelene and her family and then four more very stressful days and nights with Rob at the hospital, I was exhausted. It took me over a week to recover.

I would normally have recovered from such a grueling experience pretty quickly. However, because ten years had passed since the accident, I had to admit I was getting older. Not good. I sure hoped we got all of the medical dramas worked out before I was too old to be of any help!

Rob studied very hard and on April 22, 2005, he graduated from Brigham Young University with a Master's in Accounting.

Rob's BYU graduation

He spent the summer and fall studying for the Certified Public Accounting (CPA) exams. He needed to pass all four sections of the exam to become a CPA. Rob accepted a job with KPMG, an international accounting firm. He took a position in the Orange County, California, office. He hoped to have his CPA before he started working there full time in October.

After several trips from Utah to California trying to find a condominium to buy, Rob finally found one that would work for him. The bathroom in the condo had to be remodeled to be wheelchair-accessible, but once that was completed he moved to Irvine, California, in August. Kent stayed with Rob as his PCA for the first four weeks to help him get adjusted. After Kent flew back to Utah for school, Rob began working for KPMG on October 10, 2005. By November 2006, he passed all four parts of the CPA exam on his first attempt.

When Rob received his first paycheck from KPMG, his Social Security checks stopped, as well as his insurance with us. As a result, if Rob had a PCA, he'd have to hire and pay for one himself. Mark and I hoped Rob would find a PCA to help him, but he decided to try living completely on his own first. If that didn't work, then he would hire a PCA.

Rob lived on the West Coast, and I felt like he couldn't have lived any further away from Boston. He was completely on his own in a new state, a new city, a new home, with a new job, and without a roommate or PCA. How would he be able to do everything by himself? He couldn't cook, and he had never done his own laundry. I worried about him every day.

As it turned out, Rob found ways to take care of his needs. He had cold cereal for breakfast, ate out for lunch, and cooked prepared meals in his microwave oven for dinner. He learned how to do his own laundry, dishes, and clean up after himself, as well. Mark and I were very impressed with Rob's efforts to fend for himself, but we still worried about him.

What if his wheelchair needed repair? Suppose his van broke down? Since the fire in the van's floor years before, it was no longer reliable. And what if he got sick? Who would be there to take care of him? I thought of endless problems he could face, and I was too far away to be able to reach him in a hurry. Again, with no other choice, I had to put Rob in the hands of God and pray that he would *somehow* be taken care of.

Looking back now, Mark and I are amazed at the personal progress Rob made after leaving home. With his sheer determination and blessings from the Lord, our fears have never materialized.

CHAPTER **30**

REED HAD BEGUN attending Bentley University in January 1997. After five years of college, most students would normally have graduated. But Reed was able to take only one or two classes each semester. Even though he went to college all year long (including summers), sometimes it was really hard for him to keep up in his classes because of illness, operations, and other problems. As a result, by 2002, Reed was only beginning his junior year at Bentley.

Our family had just returned from a trip to Utah for Natalie's wedding, when I got up one morning to help the nurse suction Reed's lungs and noticed that something wasn't right. Reed's secretions were bright red, his temperature was gradually creeping up, and his spasms looked more like jolts. When the nurse and I suctioned his lungs again a little later and the mucus was still very red, I called the doctor. He told us to take Reed to the ER.

After some testing, the doctor reported that Reed had pneumonia (fluid inside his lungs) and possibly effusion (fluid in the lining outside of his lungs). Reed was admitted into the hospital and given IV antibiotics while other tests were run on his blood, urine, and sputum to see if something else was contributing to his problems.

It was a good thing we called the doctor and got Reed to the hospital when we did, because he ended up being very sick. At first, as was often the case, we thought he would be there only for a day or two, but we found out the next day that

Reed had a UTI (urinary tract infection), pneumonia, effusion, and blood poisoning! I blinked. It all came on so fast that we were shocked when Reed ended up being in the hospital for nine days, and of course, I was there with him every day.

At school that semester Reed had been taking biology and finance, but the semester was almost over and finals were coming up. The day he got out of the hospital, we stopped at home for his books and drove straight to Bentley. Reed was worried about how far behind he was, so we went to both professors and found out exactly what we needed to do to catch up. By the time we arrived home, it was 10:00 p.m.

A few weeks later we woke up one morning to find Reed's ankle really swollen. We wondered if he had phlebitis (a blood clot) or maybe even thrombosis (a moving blood clot with the potential of traveling to his heart and causing either a stroke or a heart attack). I called the doctor and, as usual, we were told to go to the ER.

After various tests and x-rays, we learned that Reed's ankle was broken. What? None of us could think of a time he had bumped or banged it. How could it have been broken? Later we found out that when our PCA was doing Reed's electro-stimulation one day, he accidentally put the machine settings on the shoulder channel instead of the calf mode. Apparently the contraction was so strong that it broke Reed's ankle. Wow! How could we ever anticipate something like that? As a result of the break, Reed was checked for osteoporosis, and unfortunately the test came back positive.

The doctor couldn't put a regular cast on Reed's ankle, because if the cast was too tight Reed wouldn't be able to tell us if he felt pressure points. He could potentially get a pressure sore without anyone knowing. Instead of a cast, the doctor used a splint: a firm piece of plastic that went down the back of Reed's calf, to his ankle, and under his foot. Then he used an Ace bandage to secure the splint. Before leaving the ER we made an appointment with an orthopedist (bone doctor) for a week later.

While we were in the ER we found out that Reed had another UTI, so we got a prescription for Furadantin to treat the infection. At home two days later Reed seemed particularly groggy and he didn't make much sense when he spoke. When he asked me for the wrong medications, I asked him if he wanted me to call the doctor. Unlike usual he said, "Yes," so I knew something was wrong; Reed never wanted me to call the doctor! At the ER we learned that on top of Reed's broken ankle and UTI, he also had pneumonia again.

A member of our church congregation was brought in with heart problems while Reed was still at the hospital ER. When Reed was settled, I slipped over to offer my support. During our conversation the man said, "I wish I had as strong a faith as you do."

I hastily replied, "No, you don't. You wouldn't want to go through what it takes to have this much faith!"

He laughed in agreement as I left to be with Reed. That time Reed was in the hospital for three days.

The following week Reed and I went to see the orthopedist. X-rays were taken again and we met with the doctor, who told us that there wasn't anything he could do for Reed's broken ankle. Now that seemed pretty strange to me, so I questioned him: "Is this an old break or a new one?"

"I don't know," was all he said.

Then I asked, "What would account for the swelling?"

Again, he didn't have an answer. The previous week I had tried to schedule a bone density test for Reed, but I was told that the first available appointment was two months away.

When I asked the doctor if there was any way he could help us get an earlier appointment he said, "No," and that was all. Reed and I were frustrated and annoyed.

Even though the doctor was concerned with skin breakdown, he had his nurse get Reed a boot-style cast. I knew however, that with the boot we could easily check for pressure sores because we could take the boot off and put it back on again.

Away from Reed the doctor explained to me, "Reed doesn't really need the boot, but people get mad if they don't go home with something." What was up with this guy? At home Reed got moved around so much that I was pretty sure he should have better protection for his ankle. Reed and I felt like the appointment had been a complete waste of time, and we were disgusted with the doctor's bedside manner. After that appointment we changed to a different orthopedist.

During Bentley's spring break in March of 2003, Reed's health was still poor, so we decided to take a few day trips instead of one big road trip like we had previous years. Reed, his PCA, and Mark and I were on our way to the Museum of Science in Boston one afternoon when we hit a couple of dips and a pothole in the road. The dips got Reed's wheelchair rocking, and when we hit the pothole the whole back of the chair suddenly broke, laying Reed flat on his back. He had really been looking forward to the trip, but we had to turn around and go back home.

We carefully got Reed out of the van, and I immediately took the wheelchair to get it repaired. It was getting old, so the repairman suggested using the spare parts from some old wheelchairs he had there at his shop to upgrade it. I thought that was a great idea. I drove back home while the repairs were made over the weekend. Monday morning I got a call from the repairman saying that our insurance company wouldn't pay for used parts, and if he had to order new parts it could take up to six weeks! We couldn't have Reed stuck in bed for that long just because of a broken chair, so we decided to pay for the used spare parts ourselves. As a result, I picked up the wheelchair that same afternoon.

In the meantime, when one of Reed's nurses did range of motion exercises on him, she felt something different when she moved his shoulder. Reed said it seemed to be very stiff and sore. Since he couldn't feel, we decided to take him to the ER to make sure nothing was injured from his wheelchair breaking. The ER technician took some x-rays, told us nothing was broken, and sent Reed home with some Motrin.

Over the weekend, however, Reed began feeling more pain and discomfort. His pain medication wasn't helping enough, and on Sunday Reed wanted to go back to the hospital. Mark reminded him that nothing much happens in the hospital over a weekend, so he decided to wait. Sunday evening Reed's pain continued to escalate, and his shoulder had swollen so much that it looked like he'd been lifting weights.

Monday morning I took Reed to the hospital to have his shoulder checked out again. I usually went into the radiology room with Reed when he had x-rays taken, but this time the technician asked me to wait outside while they x-rayed Reed's shoulder and, not wanting to cause a hassle, I consented. Unfortunately when Reed was rolled out of the room he told me that one of the technicians had raised his sore arm way back over his head and even weighed it down with a bag of sand or something like that to keep it still while they took the x-ray. Reed also told me that the technician repositioned his shoulder and arm at least twice and he had heard some cracking and grinding. When the new x-rays were read, the ER doctor came into the room and told us that Reed's shoulder was broken. This was the result of a careless x-ray technician.

After the doctor left, I closed the door, put my arms around Reed as best I could, and together we wept. We had gone to the hospital for help and ended up with another serious injury. We were both terribly discouraged.

Reed's shoulder continued to swell during the day and his pain got worse. In the early evening, he was given a CAT scan to determine if there were any additional injuries. There weren't any. The ER doctor put Reed's arm in a sling and wrapped a swathe around him to keep his arm stationary against his body. Once the doctor read the CAT scan Reed would be released from the hospital and we could go home.

After waiting several hours for the results of the scan, Reed got very impatient. He asked me to go find out what was taking so long, and I did. The nursing assistant at the front desk told me that she was waiting for the doctor to call her back. After a while Reed persuaded me to ask again, and when I did I got the same answer. Reed began begging me every five minutes to check to see if the results of the CAT scan were back, so I went to find someone to help us. When I finally found a nurse, I told her that there was no excuse for such a long delay. She told me that she had already paged the doctor, so I asked her, "How many times?"

"Two," was her reply.

I was so irritated that the doctor had been paged only twice in so many hours that I said, "Well, page him again! Or better yet, go find him, or I will!"

It was just before midnight when we finally got the reading of the CAT scan. After a very long and annoying day, Reed and I headed home. As we pulled out of the hospital parking lot, I tried to drive very carefully so Reed's shoulder wouldn't get jerked around and cause him more pain. But before I had gone one hundred yards, the driver in the car behind me began honking her horn at me. I continued going slowly for Reed, and moved over so the lady could pass. There was plenty of room, with only a few cars on the road that late at night. Instead of passing me, though, she just continued blaring on her horn. Suddenly I'd had enough! My patience was long gone and the shrill honking grated on my nerves. I stopped the van, jumped out, and ran back to her car, screaming at her as I pounded on her window with my fists, "My son is paralyzed in a wheelchair and he has a broken shoulder! Quit honking at me!" By the look on her face, I knew she was terrified. It was a major case of road rage, but at that moment, I snapped. I just couldn't take any more.

When I explained what had happened to Mark, I felt ashamed and embarrassed. I couldn't believe that I had lost control of my emotions to the point of a roadway meltdown. In the past when I'd heard or read reports of road rage, it was hard for me to understand how someone could get so angry that they lost control. I had been very critical. Now I recognized that I had completely lost control to the point of terrorizing that poor lady, whether she was at fault or not, and the realization caused me intense feelings of guilt and remorse.

Not only that, but I felt discouraged wondering why Reed could never get positive news. Why did it seem like he was always behind the eight ball? I didn't have an answer. It took me a long time to settle down enough to fall asleep that night. I was worthless for the next several days because of my rage that night.

Reed and I were told that his shoulder would be healed in six weeks, but that didn't seem possible and I asked the doctor about it. He said, "Reed's bones aren't any different from ours, so six weeks should be fine." But by mid-May Reed had already been in the sling and swathe for eight weeks and we were told that he would need to be in them for another four weeks.

Reed's shoulder eventually healed. However, he had gone months without his range of motion exercises or therapy on his shoulder, and he lost a lot of flexibility during that time. His muscles became much weaker in his left shoulder, and Reed continues to have a lot of extra pain as a result. Many nights he can't turn on his left side due to the pain. The injury was so unnecessary.

In normal circumstances Reed had a lot of medical expenses, but when Reed or anyone else is abused by poorly trained or incompetent medical personnel it significantly increases the medical cost for all of us. I am convinced that proper medical treatment administered in the first place would go a long way in reducing the exploding national medical costs.

ᴊᴊᴊ

Mark and I had found that it was critical for us to get away every so often, so we took a trip to Hawaii. When we got home, however, we discovered that Reed's bladder hadn't been emptied often enough while we were gone, and he had gotten another UTI. While Mark and I were gone, Reed's infectious disease doctor had prescribed the antibiotic Cipro to clear up the infection, the same antibiotic that Rob had been on when he struggled with autonomic dysreflexia. The drug hadn't worked.

Since Reed had already been on Cipro for several days by the time Mark and I got home, I knew he should have been improving, but his blood pressure started getting higher and higher until it got to 205/149! Then, in a short period of time, it dropped so low that it didn't even register on the monitor.

Mark and I also noticed that whenever Reed ate anything, even a cracker, his blood pressure dropped nearly out of sight, but we didn't know why. When we asked the doctor about it, he didn't know either. We later learned that the drop in blood pressure was a side effect of one of Reed's pain medications, so we tried to minimize Reed's use of that particular medicine from then on.

CHAPTER **31**

REED CONTINUED TO get worse. Mark and I were very concerned about him. Besides that, at Reed's suggestion we had planned a family reunion in Williamsburg, Virginia, and we were all supposed to leave in two days to meet the rest of our kids there. With Reed's being so ill, we didn't know if he could travel. I tried and tried to reach Reed's doctors, but no one was available to answer my calls.

Finally, after several hours had passed, I spoke to Reed's GI doctor but, other than telling me to put some liquid Band-Aid around Reed's sore G-tube site, he couldn't help us. We decided to take Reed to the ER and had just called for an ambulance when his infectious disease doctor called. She said to have the ER call her when Reed got to the hospital, so I sent Reed off in the ambulance. When I could, I preferred to drive my own car because I never knew how long Reed might stay at the hospital, and that way I could come home if I needed to.

I arrived shortly after Reed and I was surprised to see his infectious disease doctor already with him when I got there. Wow! We usually had to wait for hours to make any progress. And the ER doctor who was assigned to Reed just happened to have trained at Kessler in West Orange, New Jersey, the rehab center where Christopher Reeve had gone after his accident, so he actually knew what autonomic dysreflexia was!

Apparently Reed still had a UTI; the Cipro hadn't cleared it up. I made a mental note that Reed and Rob shouldn't use

Cipro for their UTIs, and we never used it again. The doctor changed Reed's antibiotic, and we hoped he could go home in a day or two so we could still have our family reunion in Virginia.

Reed was released from the hospital the night before we were supposed to leave. He came home with a PICC (peripheral inserted central catheter) line, which was like an IV port, but the tubing was much longer. It was inserted into Reed's upper arm and threaded into one of the main veins in his chest, giving us easier access to his veins. The doctor told us to call him the next morning to let him know how Reed did during the night. Unfortunately, Reed didn't do as well as we'd hoped, because his blood pressure was too high. Mark and I decided that Reed was too unstable to travel.

It took a tremendous amount of time and effort, but we finally got all our kids' airline tickets changed to fly into Boston instead of Williamsburg, Virginia. Then we had the family reunion at home, where Reed had nurses every day and his doctors were close by.

We all had a wonderful time together at the reunion, and everyone was happy to be with Reed. He still had a lot of problems with his blood pressure, but I ran his IV meds every day and we hoped he'd be better soon. Unfortunately, by the time our reunion ended, Reed's blood pressure was over 200 again. After talking to the doctor, we decided that Reed needed to go to the ER, and I called for an ambulance.

It was a sad and difficult way to end our family reunion, each one having to say good-bye to Reed as he took off in the ambulance. Most of our kids would be leaving the next day and wouldn't see him again for quite a while. Reed's sisters were all crying and his brothers-in-law had tears in their eyes, too.

Reed and I got to the ER at 11:00 p.m. and his blood pressure had gone up to 232/169. Although he still had a PICC line in his arm, the nurses couldn't seem to draw any blood from it. They poked Reed at least a dozen times trying to get another line in, but every attempt was unsuccessful. The doctor was almost ready to put in a central line (tubing that attached to one of the large veins which fed into Reed's heart), when another doctor came in and was able to draw some blood from Reed's femoral artery in his lower abdomen.

Reed was in a lot of pain in the ER, but he couldn't have any medicine until certain tests were administered. When he finally got a shot of Demerol for the pain, his blood pressure went so low that he couldn't get any more until his blood pressure came back up to a normal range. As his blood pressure was on its way back up again, a lot of sick people arrived at the ER. When Reed was in horrible pain again, the nurses were too busy with the other patients to get more Demerol for him.

Reed tried to be patient, but finally he cried as he asked me, "Why does it have to be so bad and why does it have to hurt so much? This pain is killing me!"

His head was ready to explode, his back really hurt, and his stomach was upset. Pretty soon he felt like everything hurt. Over the next several hours Reed's blood pressure went from 68/29 to 164/130 and back down again to 94/34. The pulse oximeter attached to his finger, which reads the amount of oxygen in the blood, registered in the low 90s instead of the normal high 90s, 100 being the best possible. Finally at 5:30 a.m. we were told that Reed was going to be admitted into the hospital when a bed became available. Why was I not surprised? We almost always had to wait for a bed and sometimes it was over twenty-four hours. While we waited, the nurse gave Reed another shot of Demerol and he was finally able to relax a little.

The results of the blood test showed that Reed's potassium level was too high, which could cause an irregular heartbeat, so he was given some insulin and other medications to lower the potassium. Reed was in the hospital for five days, and by the time we got him back home Rob was the only one of his siblings still there after the reunion, and he was leaving two days later to go back to BYU.

Since Reed felt a little better the next day, we went to dinner and shopping for Rob's last night at home. Mark took Rob to the airport early the next morning. I was still asleep when the PCA knocked at my bedroom door and told me that one of Reed's testicles and his groin were causing him a lot of pain. Groggily, I told her to give him more pain medicine.

In the meantime, Mark got home from the airport and went straight upstairs to take a nap before going to work. A little while later we were both awakened by another knock at the door. The PCA told us that Reed was in the shower in horrible pain and wanted to see us. It was a good thing Mark had come home after taking Rob to the airport instead of going directly to work, because we had to get Reed to the ER as soon as possible and Mark could finish Reed's shower much quicker than the nurse or I could. But even with Mark's hurrying, Reed was crying out in pain. I blinked.

Shortly after Mark and I got Reed back into bed, Reed began repeating short sentences over and over. He'd say things like, "I don't know what's going on with my body," or "I just never feel good anymore." He kept saying, "It hurts so much; I hate this so much," and "My testicle hurts so much; my head hurts so much." But Mark and I were even more worried when Reed started to call us "Mommy" and "Daddy." He'd say, "Mommy my back hurts so much," and "Daddy I feel like my testicle is going to explode. Please, please, please. Mommy, Mommy."

Mark and I suspected that Reed was delirious with pain. The nurse and I quickly got him dressed and I drove him to the hospital. Mark followed us in his car so he could go straight to work after Reed was settled. All of the way to the hospital Reed continued his moaning and saying, "Mommy, hurry. Hurry. Heavenly Father, Jesus, take the pain away." It broke my heart and I pleaded with the Lord to ease his pain.

When Reed was settled in the ER a lot of tests were run but they all came back negative. Mark and I realized that when Reed went to the hospital in a lot of pain, the doctors just gave him more medicine to help his body relax and calm down. Since all of the tests were negative, we figured that if all the ER was going to do was give Reed more pain relievers, we could do that, so we took him home. Reed had been in the hospital three times in three weeks and we were all tired of it. For some odd reason Reed's testicle became extremely painful after the blood was drawn from his femoral artery, but Mark and I found that we were able to control his pain with a little more medication and frequent prayers.

At the ER we noticed that when Reed was given a powerful shot of medication he would fall asleep and generally feel somewhat better when he woke up. We didn't have those powerful drugs at home, but we did have Oxycodone and Percocet. Most people have to be careful not to overdose on medications like these since all opiates suppress the respiratory system. A person overdosing could fall asleep and stop breathing. This wasn't a concern for Reed because the ventilator breathed for him. When his pain became unbearable he could take enough of these strong medicines to go to sleep without worrying if he was going to wake up.

Over the next year Reed and I took many more trips to the ER, trying to figure out why he felt so terrible. In between those times, we resolved his pain issues with stronger medication. Eventually we learned that Reed had diabetes and would need insulin the rest of his life. I guess we weren't totally surprised, since Mark's grandparents on both his father's and mother's sides of the family struggled with diabetes, but we were terribly concerned.

One reason Reed probably got diabetes at such a young age was due to his various medications. Many of them had side effects of elevated blood sugar. And getting awakened every few hours to be turned disturbed Reed's sleep patterns, which could also raise blood sugar levels.

Although we didn't know if we could keep Reed stabilized at home, we did know that if he was put in any other facility he wouldn't live very long. He just couldn't get the specialized care in a long-term care facility that he received at home with the nurses he'd had for over a decade, and Mark's and my constant love and dedication to him.

◗◗◗◗

A new semester was beginning and Reed was looking forward to his Accounting 260 course at Bentley. He was also looking forward to getting out of the house on a regular basis. We had a new PCA that fall, so on the first day of classes I asked him to drive the van. I went along to show him how to get to Bentley and what his responsibilities were while Reed was at school. We got Reed loaded up, locked down, and on our way to Bentley with plenty of time to spare. We wanted to arrive early enough to introduce Reed to the professor. But as we turned the corner out of our cul-de-sac, we heard a loud crack as one of the supports on the back of Reed's chair broke again. The look on Reed's face said it all: "What next?"

We turned around and hurried back home. I ran to our neighbor's house to see if anyone could help us get Reed out of the van, into the house, and back in bed. Fortunately, their two teenage sons were home and came right over to help. While we were getting Reed out of the van, the other back support on the wheelchair broke, putting him in a reclined position while five of us tried to get him into the house. Reed's PCA stayed with him at home while I drove to Bentley to meet his professor and take notes so he wouldn't get behind.

I'd had a very hard year with both Reed's and Rob's health, and I was so overwhelmed that I cried as I drove to Bentley that day. I called each of my daughters, telling them what had happened, and they cried with me. I felt like I was barely hanging on to the last strands of my rope and that at any moment I would fall into that bottomless pit of discouragement, despair, and self-pity. Then while I was driving, I decided I needed to pray.

I prayed vocally, which I never did when saying my personal prayers, and talked to the Lord about how I felt. I told Him how tired and discouraged I was and that I didn't understand why so many bad things continued to happen to Reed. Wasn't being paralyzed enough? Why did Reed have to suffer with so much pain and so many trials? I told the Lord that I still knew that He was in control of things, but that I just couldn't understand why Reed's trials were so hard. As I drove I prayed and cried to the Lord, asking Him to either lighten my burdens or strengthen my back to be able to get through all that was required of me.

As I continued to drive I realized that I needed an attitude adjustment. I began thinking of the blessings we'd received that day. We'd been blessed that we were so close to home when Reed's chair broke. Our neighbors were able to help us get Reed out of the van, into the house, and into bed. And we had left home early enough that after taking care of Reed I still had time to get to Bentley for his class. I began to be more thankful and decided to pray vocally again, this time thanking the Lord for His blessings to us. I thanked my Heavenly Father for my Savior, and that He had already suffered for all of our trials and hardships, so He knew how to comfort us. I thanked Him for my testimony of the gospel of Jesus Christ and for the guidance of the Holy Ghost. Then I closed my prayer and went to class.

On my way home a lot of thoughts ran through my head; one in particular was: "Focus on the blessings." I grabbed a notepad from my purse and wrote down those words. I couldn't stop thinking about them, so I wrote more of my thoughts and ideas. By the time I got home from school that night I'd written a poem. Perhaps later I could put the poem to music.

Focus on the Blessings

Looking back the past twelve months, my life has really changed.
Everything that once seemed good has all been rearranged.
Every day I've prayed for strength and watched for peace ahead,
But bad gets worse and I cry out, "I wish that I was dead!"

"Oh how much longer can I go on?" I ask the Lord, "How long?"

And all I hear inside my head is, "Patience child, hold on.
I know that you can't see me now, and yet I'm always
here.
Although you may not understand, I have a plan, my dear.

You must think about the good things and trust I know
what's best.
Just think about the good things, and I will do the rest."
The answer came so clearly, right there inside my head,
And I knew exactly what to do when I was tormented.

I focus on the blessings the Lord has given me.
Focus on the blessings, for that is when I see
That when my mind is full of doubt and I just want to
scream and shout,
If I focus on the blessings, the Lord will give me peace.

Now when I'm overburdened and life seems so unfair
And I begin to wonder if Father is really there,
I gather up my burden and lay it at His throne
And pray with deep thanksgiving for everything He's
done....

When I focus on the blessings, the Lord will give me
peace.

From, Focus On the Blessings, words by Sheryl Nixon,
2003, music by Kent Nixon, 2010

Now I know that writing a poem or words to a song
most likely wouldn't do a thing for anyone else, but I was
certain that Heavenly Father knew it would help me. He
had heard my prayers and was sending the comfort and sup-

port I desperately needed to be able to continue on with my life's difficult journey. Truly, I had "cast my burden upon the Lord," and He had sustained me. I just hoped that I could help Reed feel some peace and comfort as well.

Over the next several days as I drove to Bentley to take notes for Reed, I continued to feel the Lord's strength and my spiritual connection returning. It had been ten years since I had started writing my song "You Shall Have Peace in Me," but I still hadn't finished it. I loved the melody and thought the words I'd written were beautiful, but I hadn't been able to make any progress on the verses. However, during my drive back and forth to Reed's classes, I felt peace filling my mind and my senses as beautiful music began playing in my head. Then, like the bright rays of sunlight breaking through the storm clouds in my mind, the lyrics wrapped themselves around me, bringing warmth and love that flowed from the top of my head down to my feet. I had prayed for strength and the Lord sent my song, *my* spiritual connection. I dedicated it to Reed.

You Shall Have Peace in Me

Can you tell me where to turn for peace? Somehow I've lost my way.
And it's so hard to understand the pain I have to face each day.
I try to gather strength and courage to help me carry on,
But it seems insufficient when day is finally done.

Can you tell me where to turn for peace? Sometimes I feel alone.
And though I give all that I have to give, I can't make it on my own.

I want to feel the Holy Spirit to help me make it through.
I've read and pondered scriptures; Lord, tell me what to
do.

"Walk in the meekness of My spirit, and you shall have
peace in Me.
When the night is dark and full of sorrow, I'll hold you
tenderly.
I'll bear you up as on eagles' wings if you wait patiently.
Fear not little child, you shall have peace in Me."

Could it be He could lighten my load?
How I yearn to know such peace.
So I pray with faith that through Him
My own strength will increase.

Now I know where I can turn for peace. I think I understand.
Difficulties will not hold me back when I'm holding Thy
hand.
Though I may not be freed from challenge and still must
give my all,
As long as Thou art with me, I know I will stand tall

And walk in the meekness of Thy spirit and I shall have
peace in Thee....

From, You Shall Have Peace in Me, Sheryl Nixon, 2003

I couldn't believe it! I felt as if I'd gone from listening to
the discord of musical instruments tuning up on stage before a
concert to the magnificence, splendor, and beautiful harmony
of the full orchestra. The clear, sweet tone of every instrument
melodically and completely filled my mind, body, and spirit

with a joy I had not yet experienced. Finally, I knew peace through the Lord's spirit and joy from singing the song I had longed for! I felt complete both spiritually and emotionally. None of our circumstances had changed, but with the help of the Lord I felt able to continue on with my incredible journey as a woman, a wife, and a mother.

CHAPTER 32

DURING THE YEARS following the accident, Mark and I were not spared our own health problems. In November of 2000, Mark and I had our yearly physicals. My appointment was first and I checked out okay. Mark's appointment was the following week, so before I left the office, I asked the doctor to give Mark a good work-over. Mark's family had a history of heart disease and diabetes, and I needed to have him around for a long time.

We found out that Mark had a hole in his heart: a congenital birth defect. He hadn't noticed any symptoms, but the doctor told him that his heart was just to the point where symptoms would begin to appear. Unfortunately, the damage that had already been done was irreversible, and any further damage couldn't be repaired either. Mark needed open heart surgery to patch the hole in his heart, or else within fifteen years he would be seriously disabled and in a wheelchair, or dead.

I blinked.

Mark and I were shocked, but we quickly realized what a blessing we'd been given. For the past four years Mark had been given stress tests during his physicals and nothing had shown up. But this time the doctor had given him a more detailed test and discovered the hole. Mark was still healthy and the surgery wasn't immediately necessary, so after the holidays were over he had open heart surgery on January 11, 2001, and the surgeon told me that it went well.

In 2002, while Mark and I were visiting relatives, Mark ended up in the hospital again with severe pain. At first the doctor thought there was a problem with Mark's heart, since he'd had open heart surgery the year before, but it turned out to be his gall bladder. Mark didn't have it taken out right then because we were far away from home, but we were told to keep a close eye on it. For several years Mark seemed to be doing fine until after another serious attack he finally had surgery to remove his gallbladder.

During Bentley's spring break in 2005, Reed had been planning to go to Cooperstown, New York, to the Baseball Hall of Fame. When the time arrived, however, he wasn't feeling well enough for such a big trip, so we decided to take some day trips during the week instead. The first day of the break Mark, Reed, and I had planned to drive to Connecticut to see the Pequot Indian Museum at Foxwoods. Reed was feeling too lightheaded to make the trip, so we went to a movie that night instead.

The next day Reed felt better and we decided to go to the museum after all. One of the exhibits there was set up to look like an outside Indian village, with teepees, uneven ground, and all. Reed had a hard time steering his wheelchair because all four of his wheels weren't touching the ground at the same time. Mark took the heavy wheelchair out of gear and steered Reed and his chair (almost four hundred pounds) through the exhibit. By the time we got home, Mark told me that his back was pretty sore from pushing Reed.

A month before, while Mark was lifting Reed into bed, he'd injured his back. Since then it had gotten better, but it wasn't completely healed. The day after our trip to Connecticut, Mark's back really hurt. He went to a massage therapist that afternoon to try to loosen it up. However, the next morning, he was in such excruciating pain that I took him to the doctor. Mark had inflammation of the sciatic nerve and he was put on anti-inflammatory drugs and medicine to ease his pain.

Mark went back to work, but he was still in a lot of pain. He finally had an MRI, which showed that he had a fragmented disc in his back. We were told that he should either have surgery or physical therapy. We opted for physical therapy, which helped quite a bit, but Mark still has to be very careful with his back.

The heart, gallbladder, and back weren't Mark's only problems. We also discovered that he had prostate cancer. He had his prostate removed and is now cancer-free. Mark and I often joke about his "losing too many 'optional' organs." I'm just thankful that he's still around.

And what about my health? Remember, when the accident happened I was struggling with fibromyalgia and depression. Well, I seemed to have pretty stable health until September 7, 2005, when I was outside in the backyard painting our shed. Stepping off the ladder wrong, I broke my ankle. I knew it was broken because my right foot was pointing sideways. Mark was at Bentley for the first day of classes that semester and he wasn't home to help me. Fortunately, I had the phone outside with me and I called my neighbor. She grabbed another neighbor and they both came over to help. Seeing my condition, they called 911 and we waited for the ambulance together. Thank heaven for good neighbors!

Strange, I had ridden to UMASS in ambulances so many times with Reed and Rob, but I'd never gone for myself. My ankle and foot had gone numb so I wasn't in horrible pain, which was a huge blessing. When I got to the ER the doctor gave me some morphine and then quickly snapped my foot back into place. Yee-ouw-ee! Did that ever hurt!

Two hours later I had ten or so x-rays taken of my ankle and foot. The x-rays showed that I had displaced my fibula (small leg bone), cracked the inside of my ankle, and chipped some bone off my heel. I was put under anesthesia and the bones were re-set. When I woke up I had a soft cast on my foot, ankle and leg. I had to use the restroom, so the nurse wheeled my cot next to the ER bathroom, got me a pair of crutches, and helped me into the restroom. Then she left me alone for some privacy.

When I was finished I used the crutches to get over to the door, but one of my crutches slipped on a piece of paper towel that had been left on the floor. I hadn't noticed it until it was too late. When I realized I was going to fall I tried to avoid landing on my broken ankle. Instead, I leaned forward and hit the door handle with my head. When the nurse asked if I was all right, I said no, but because I was leaning against the door she couldn't get in. She finally got through the door and helped me stand up straight. My head hurt where I had bumped it, so I rubbed it and saw blood on my hand. Then I saw blood dripping from my head to the floor and I knew I was in trouble. The nurse got me back to my room and cleaned me up, and the doctor put four stitches in my forehead. I looked like I'd been in a serious car accident instead of just stepping off a ladder wrong.

The doctor told me I needed surgery to put a plate and screws in my ankle to hold the bones together until they healed. I wouldn't be able to put any weight on my leg and foot for six weeks! Oh no! How could I take care of Reed?

One night, shortly thereafter, I had a dream that was vivid enough for me to remember. I dreamed I was unprepared for school and hauling cement in a little red wagon. My arms were full of things but I needed to carry more, and I was trying to muster the strength to do it. When I awakened I knew that my dream was a reflection of my life at that point in time. I felt unprepared for the future, whatever it would bring, especially where Reed and Rob were concerned. My load was heavy with life's trials and responsibilities; I needed to increase my faith and trust in God. I slowly made progress, and I continued trying to help myself and my family survive.

At home I stayed on the main level of the house in Rob's room, on his hospital bed. I showered in his bathroom, sitting on Reed's shower chair, and I even used Rob's spare wheelchair to get around during the day. In the van when we drove to church I sat right next to Reed, like Rob had done. Then, sitting through several hours of Sunday meetings, my bottom really hurt and I could understand the pain that resulted from staying in one position too long. Although Rob was paralyzed, he still had some sensation and often experienced what is sometimes called "fire butt" from sitting in one position too long. Now I knew exactly what Rob felt, but he suffered through it all day, every day!

The first week after my accident I took some pain medicine that had been prescribed for me. I had wondered earlier why Reed was always so uncomfortable even though he took several strong pain medications. Now I completely understood. I had always thought that the pain pills took away the pain, such as when I took Excedrin for a migraine headache and the headache went away. However, after breaking my ankle, I realized that the pain pills only took the edge off; they never took the pain away entirely. Besides, the side effects of feeling lightheaded, anxious, and drowsy were almost worse than the pain itself, so after that first week I just took ibuprofen.

Another important thing I learned from my accident was

to cheerfully accept the help people offered me. Now I understood how the boys felt when the people who helped them didn't always do things the way they wanted them done. I had to learn to graciously accept the help that others offered me, regardless of how I preferred having things done.

One of my most difficult challenges was not being able to drive. There were so many things I needed to get done. But after breaking my ankle, I had to ask someone to drive me whenever I had to go somewhere, such as my physical therapy appointments three days a week. Mark worked all day long and when he got home I didn't have the heart to ask him to go grocery shopping, mow the lawn, harvest the garden, and mop the floor. Thankfully, my wonderful neighbors and friends took care of those things for me.

Although I was disappointed at being stuck in bed most of the time, I tried to focus on constructive things I could do to pass the time. During the first year after the boys' accident Mark had recorded some audio tapes on his way to and from work and the hospital. I decided to transcribe them so we could have a written record of his thoughts and feelings during those early days. Day in and day out I listened to those tapes, writing down everything Mark had said, and I felt like he was in my room talking to me every day.

I figured out that it took about six hours for me to transcribe one tape, which ended up being about thirty-six handwritten pages. Since I had thirteen tapes, it took most of the six weeks I was in bed for me to finish transcribing them. But what I hadn't realized was that after the six weeks in bed were over I had to have a cast on for another six weeks! I still couldn't drive!

For those additional six weeks I got wrapped up in taking the accident-related information out of my journals, and

I began to write the story of Reed and Rob and our family's incredible journey for a book. When Reed found out that I was writing a book about Rob and himself he said, "Wow! I can hardly wait to see what happens next!"

He was always quick to make a joke.

Being laid up with a broken ankle gave me insight to a tiny part of what Reed and Rob had gone through for the past ten years. I had gained a new appreciation for their courage and determination.

CHAPTER **33**

APRIL 4, 2005, was the ten-year anniversary of our kids' accident, and we could hardly believe we'd already gotten that far into our unexpected journey. One moment we felt like we were just getting started on our uncharted path, and the next moment we felt like our years together as a family before the accident were only a dream. Any discussion about our family activities was categorized by "before the accident" and "after the accident." But at least, after ten years, our lives were much more stable and we had a routine that was pretty consistent.

After so many years of hard use, Reed's wheelchair was literally falling apart. Two years before, Mark and I had noticed that the chair was getting old and we'd started the process of getting him a new one. We were working with one particular wheelchair company and had already received the doctor's prescription and the nurse's letter of evaluation, so we sent the information to our insurance company. When our insurance company had some additional questions, they called to speak to the evaluation nurse. But she wasn't one of our in-home nurses.

As it turned out, that particular nurse had moved and left the company she was with, so she couldn't answer the questions. As a result, our insurance company made us start all over again with a new letter of evaluation and prescription. Starting over would take months because it took a long time to get an appointment with an evaluation nurse. And the prescription took extra time to write because it had to be worded in a particular way for the insurance company to accept it.

The next company we worked with got all of Reed's information, but halfway through the process they decided everything was too complicated for them to continue. A third company took on the project, but they also backed out. We finally had to go back to the company who built Reed's original wheelchair, but our insurance had changed since the accident and our current insurance policy didn't cover that company.

Several months later we found a company in Connecticut that got all of the specifications for the chair, had it built, and was ready to deliver it. When Mark asked if the TTK was hooked up and ready to go as well, they said, "What's a TTK?" We were so disappointed. Apparently both the chair and the TTK were approved by our insurance company, but the wheelchair company thought they were two separate orders. We had to wait another six months to get Reed's new wheelchair with his TTK drive system. By that time Reed's old wheelchair was literally held together with duct tape and we were afraid it would be useless before we got the replacement. In April 2006, almost three years from the time we started the process, Reed finally received his brand-new chair.

Reed's new wheelchair was a big improvement over the old one. With a shorter wheel-base and six wheels instead of four, he was able to spin on a dime. The new chair allowed Reed to get into smaller spaces, such as some of the elevators at school. The chair also had shocks for a better ride and because it held a much smaller ventilator, Reed didn't rock as much when he was in the van and went over bumps and dips in the road.

A seat elevator on this new chair raised Reed up to ten inches higher, too. Now, instead of always having to look up at people, he could have conversations face to face. At sporting events when the crowd got excited and stood up, Reed could actually raise up his seat and see what was going on instead of having to imagine what was happening like he used to.

꧁꧂

For several months I had been praying that Rob would find a wife, or that she would find him, or that they would find each other. Then in October 2005, I learned that Rob had a girlfriend: a nineteen-year-old young lady from Utah. Rob was robbing the cradle!

Katie Eliza Donaldson was the oldest daughter of Craig and Alice Donaldson. Craig had been Reed and Rob's youth leader and advisor at our church in Massachusetts before the accident. The Donaldsons lived in Northborough for two years and had moved away several months before the accident. At the time, Rob was sixteen and Katie was only nine, and they didn't know each other. Now, however, they had grown up. Rob was twenty-six and Katie was nineteen.

Mark and I had kept in touch with Craig and Alice over the years through Christmas cards. Whenever they were in town on business or vacation, we got together for lunch or dinner. When Rob moved to California and was living there alone, Craig found out and invited Rob to a family reunion his family was having in Southern California that year. When Rob and Katie met at the reunion it was love at first sight!

*Rob & Katie sailing at Donaldson Family Reunion with
Katie's uncle, Paul (left) and father, Craig (right)*

Since Katie lived in Utah, she and Rob began their relationship by e-mailing each other. Before long, Rob's phone
bills were skyrocketing with the two of them on the phone
nearly every day. Then it got to the point where either Rob
flew to Utah to be with Katie every other weekend, or Katie
flew to California to be with Rob. Before we knew it they
were engaged to be married. I blinked.

I knew my prayers had been answered. Mark and I were
thrilled, but we worried about Craig and Alice. Although they
knew us all very well and had admired Reed and Rob for years,
we didn't know how they would feel about their daughter mar-
rying someone in a wheelchair, whether it was Rob or anyone
else. We were sure that this wasn't what they had been planning
for their daughter. Even though Rob was pretty self-sufficient,
there were many things in life that he would not be able to do,
and that might limit Katie's experiences, too.

When Katie's spring semester was over she packed up and moved to her aunt's house in California for the summer to be closer to Rob. Living near each other really helped her see more of what Rob's day-to-day life was like, and her parents were especially glad that Katie was getting a clear understanding of what her life would be like, being married to Rob.

During that same summer, Mark, Reed, and I flew to Utah for a couple of family reunions, and while we were there we stayed at Raelene's house. One afternoon Craig dropped by to pick up Rob's shower chair and Mark and I were able to visit with him for a little while. We were very pleased when he told us that he and Alice "were happy that our families bumped into each other in Massachusetts." We had worried that Katie's parents were unhappy with her decision to marry Rob, but talking with Craig that day eased our concerns.

Katie moved back to Utah for the fall semester at BYU and was sad to be so far away from Rob again. Rob also missed Katie a lot and he began checking with KPMG to see if there were any available positions in their Salt Lake City office, hoping he could transfer there to be closer to Katie.

In January 2007, Rob transferred to the Salt Lake City office of KPMG. He found an apartment with a roll-in shower that was only 1½ blocks from his office. He rented out his apartment in Irvine, California, planning to return there after he and Katie were married and after Katie graduated.

Kent was attending BYU that same January, 2007, when he met his future wife, Kayla Nicole Nauman. The two of them were engaged after Rob and Katie and married before them on May 4, 2007, in the Salt Lake Temple.

I was extremely busy addressing invitations and helping plan two weddings. Fortunately, with both of these weddings, my responsibilities as the mother of the groom weren't as complicated as when our three daughters were married. We all flew to Utah twice within three months for the weddings.

Katie and Rob set their wedding date for July 3, 2007, to be married for time and all eternity in the Mount Timpanogos Temple of The Church of Jesus Christ of Latter-day Saints. Their reception would be held that evening at the Sundance Resort in Utah.

On Friday, June 29th, Mark, Reed, our PCA, and I flew to Utah for Rob and Katie's wedding. It was a whirlwind of a trip. When we first arrived at the airport to check in, we discovered that somehow Reed's and the PCA's reservations for the airline had been canceled! It took a while to get everything sorted out and get our tickets, but after that things went pretty smoothly.

2007 Nixon Family courtesy Busath Photography

Although the days before the wedding were jammed with a grandchild's baptism, a picnic in the park, trips to the beauty salon, and chaotic family pictures, the day of the wedding was beautiful.

Rob & Katie after wedding ceremony courtesy Busath Photography

At the temple that morning my uncle performed the wedding and sealing ceremonies. I felt extremely blessed to be there with all of my children, all of their spouses, and many friends and relatives. I recognized that as a family we'd had enormous challenges and trials in our lives, but that our extraordinary wedding experience that day was one of the most wonderful blessings that the Lord had ever given us.

Sheryl & Rob after wedding courtesy Busath Photography

Today my heart is filled with joy as I sit in the Lord's sacred house
And look at each of my children, along with my eternal spouse.

The gospel plan brings families together forever, that's the principle I have learned,
But it certainly hasn't come easily, and for each of us it has to be earned.

Today my heart is filled with a peace that can only come from the Lord
For trying to keep His commandments and living each day by His word.

Now I certainly am not perfect, and I've worked through trials and strife,
But once in a while there comes a time when contentment encompasses my life.

Today is that day, and I feel a deep love for God and His son Jesus Christ
For sending me an eternal family to love and cherish all my life.

Sheryl Nixon, 2007

I will never forget Rob's and Katie's first dance at their reception that evening. Rob in his tux and Katie in her wedding gown rolled and floated across the floor in an artistic, romantic dance that had the rest of us awestruck. Katie was so graceful and Rob so handsome that as they moved to the music, many of us had tears in our eyes. There was no doubt that they were a match made in heaven.

Rob & Katie's first dance courtesy Busath Photography

CHAPTER **34**

AFTER BEING SO sick, Reed ended up not going back to school the fall semester of 2003, but he began again after the Christmas break. In the past we had sent various PCAs to school with Reed to take notes for him, but we had some who couldn't stay awake very well, some who couldn't spell very well, and some who didn't drive very well. After discussing the matter with Mark and Reed, I decided that I would take Reed to school. He was used to my driving, I stayed awake, I was a pretty good speller, and I was interested in one of his classes. I figured that it was the least I could do for Reed.

Because I had completed only one semester of college when I was young, I wasn't very knowledgeable about the subject matter of most of Reed's classes. My interests were in the arts, while his were in finance, so when his other course for the semester was Financial Analysis, I really struggled. I knew how to take pretty good notes, but without having any background on the subject, I didn't know what was important enough to write down and what wasn't, so I just tried to write as much of what the professor said as was possible. By the end of each class I was exhausted, and I still had to get Reed loaded up and then drive an hour to get home.

I felt responsible for Reed's grades because he studied from *my* notes. There were many times that he fell asleep in class, due to his heavy medications, so I was particularly nervous about getting the notes right. But I didn't just struggle with note-taking. It seemed that something always went wrong on the days we went to class. Once it was a dead battery in the van. Another time Reed's chair malfunctioned and ran him into a cement wall, breaking his big toe. It was always something. But Reed had an amazingly endless supply of patience and he helped me make it through some pretty frustrating times.

In January 2005, Reed continued his schooling at Bentley University by taking Financial Analysis II for the semester. But on the first day of class I couldn't get his van started and Reed had to stay home with the PCA. I drove to Bentley, met the professor, and took notes for Reed during class.

During the following summer semester Reed took a Revolutionary War class. One week was particularly hectic as I helped him finish his mid-term exam, prepare an in-class oral presentation, practice for a class debate, and write a final paper to turn in for the final exam. By the end of the week I was totally exhausted. Writing papers was long and tedious. It wasn't uncommon for us to sit at the computer for five hours at a time trying to complete a writing assignment.

The most difficult part in the process of typing for Reed was that he usually didn't know what he wanted to write when we sat at the computer. He had ideas but he had to think things out, put his thoughts into sentences, and then dictate them to me. There were many times when he'd have me type a sentence and then he'd think of something better. Then I'd have to go back, erase it, and type the new sentence. Other times Reed would have to stop and read certain parts of a chapter in the textbook before he could continue with the paper. Even though I was happy to help him, sometimes Reed's schoolwork really stressed me out.

In an effort to help Reed be more independent using the computer, Mark and I had purchased a voice-activated system several years before, but it took Reed so long to use it that he'd get frustrated. Often the computer didn't understand the word he said. For example, if Reed said the word "shoe," the computer might print the word two, who, or you. When an incorrect word was typed, Reed had to read a list of alternate words on the computer and say "choose two" for the second word on the list or "choose four" for the fourth word on the list. If the word Reed wanted wasn't on the list he'd have to spell the word out using the international alphabet of alpha, bravo, charlie, delta, and so forth. If I typed his papers instead of having him use voice-activation, he could move along much faster and with less frustration.

Reed took only one class a semester when he wasn't feeling very well, but when he felt better he took two classes. That was great for Reed, but it was torture for me! After taking notes for over three hours straight, my mind was frazzled and my hand ached. Many times I left class so stressed that I started to cry, but I tried to keep it to myself so Reed wouldn't feel bad. At home I often skipped dinner and went straight to my room to try to calm down.

Mark and I eventually learned about a university program that would provide and pay for students to take notes for Reed, so I wouldn't need to go with him any longer. Instead, his PCA drove him to school, waited for him, and then drove him back home.

One night I got a call from our PCA telling me that he and Reed were on their way home earlier than usual because Reed had an unexpected bowel movement. At that particular time I was still unable to put any weight on the ankle I'd broken a few weeks before, so I called our morning PCA and she came over to help get Reed into bed and cleaned up. However, Reed had fallen asleep on the way home and our

PCA couldn't get him to respond. Because he didn't want to disturb or upset me, he poked his head inside the door and got our morning PCA's attention. But when she went outside to the van to help, she couldn't get Reed to wake up either.

Recognizing that there was something wrong, I quickly got into Rob's old wheelchair, wheeled out to the van, and moved the lift up to get into the van. I tried calling Reed's name several times, but he didn't respond. His ventilator was working and no alarms were sounding, so I couldn't tell if Reed was just in a very deep sleep or if he had passed out or if something else was wrong. I blinked. My heart pounded faster and faster as I put my hands on his face and shook him while I continued yelling his name.

When I still couldn't get a response out of him I had the PCA run into the house and get me the phone so I could call 911. I started to panic, but I remembered that if I did, I wouldn't be able to think straight to know what to do for Reed. I silently prayed for strength and for help knowing what I should do. While we waited for the ambulance, I had the thought that I needed to use the AMBU bag to give more and larger breaths to Reed. I also closed his mouth so that all of the air went into his lungs instead of some leaking out of his mouth. After several breaths, Reed jerked and opened his eyes just as the ambulance pulled up.

The Emergency Medical Technician (EMT) checked all of Reed's vital signs and they were normal. He asked if we still wanted Reed to go to the hospital, but we decided that since his vital signs were fine we would just put him to bed and keep an eye on him. We could always call 911 again if necessary, but we didn't need to. Reed didn't have any residual effects from the episode, but it sure scared us.

By the time the fall 2006 semester began at Bentley,

Reed had only two classes left to graduate. However, he still had five incomplete classes from the times he was sick and couldn't finish the courses and we needed to finish them, too. Mark and I could finally see a light at the end of the tunnel regarding Reed's education, so we made a conscious effort to finish as much as we could as fast as we could, hoping that Reed could graduate in May of 2007.

Before the accident, when Reed ran a race, he'd save up a little energy so that in the last fifty yards he still had enough strength to sprint to the end, and that's exactly what he did with his classes, too. That semester Reed finished a history course called America in the Progressive Era, which completed his History Minor, and his last elective course, Business Law—and we were finally on the home stretch, racing toward the finish line. From January through April we spent innumerable hours at the computer, and one by one we ticked off each remaining incomplete he had received. After ten years in college Reed reached deep down, as he had during every race in his life, and pulled out that last bit of strength he had to reach the end.

On May 19, 2007, Reed graduated Magna Cum Laude from Bentley University with a Bachelor of Science degree in Finance.

I blinked as cameras flashed and the entire faculty, students, and guests rose to give Reed a standing ovation. I looked around and saw everyone at the graduation standing, clapping, and whistling for Reed. The whole graduation ceremony came to a stop. Mark stepped down from the faculty platform, gave Reed a big hug, and congratulated him as he presented Reed with his diploma. The race was over and Reed was declared the winner!

2007 Reed's Bentley graduation courtesy GradImages

The Race

I tighten my shoes, strap my number on,
I hear the gun go off, then everybody's gone
For the finish line.
This race is mine.

I start way too fast. I gotta pull it back,
Wait for my time 'til I'm ready to attack,
Feel the runner's high
As I pass 'em by.

The thought in my mind says I'll never be left behind.

I'm gonna win the race. No, second place won't be good
enough.
I know I'm tougher than who I was before.
And I will seize the day, put my trophy upon display,
So I can show everyone who's number one.

I wake up, my old life's gone.
Disappointment and anger I ponder, but they won't do to
get me through.
I start therapy. It makes me a little stronger.
Some of life's trials will be lifelong, but I still have life, so
I'll live it right.

The trophy by my door says I've never given up before.

I'm gonna win the race. No, second place won't be good
enough....

I know what it's like to be an "underdog."
My daddy taught me to put my faith in God.
So every goal I set with no regret will help me to the time
When I cross the line.

I'm gonna win the race....

From, The Race, Kent Mark Nixon, 2009

CHAPTER **35**

WATCHING MY SONS grow from little boys to young men was thrilling. I loved seeing them learn new skills as their bodies made the transition into adolescence. As they progressed from T-ball to Little League baseball, from elementary school's field day races to setting new high school records for their track team, my heart swelled with pride seeing them improve their abilities, and even finding new ones.

After the accident, Reed's and Rob's physical abilities became less important to me. Instead, I found great joy as I saw each of them develop strong characters, positive attitudes, and extraordinary spirits. Expectations and priorities evolved from physical growth and abilities to mental, social, emotional, and spiritual strengths. Now instead of my being the one my sons look up to, I look up to them. They have become positive examples of peace and joy in life, not only to me, but to everyone who has ever met them.

Through my experiences I now know the true meaning of peace. It does not mean to be in a place where there is no noise, trouble, or hard work. It means to be in the midst of those things and still be calm in your heart.

I have a beautiful picture of a road curving through a scenic mountain landscape. Its caption says, "A bend in the road is not the end of the road unless you fail to make the turn." My path took more than just a turn; it sent me right off the road! For a while I wallowed in self-pity. I wandered blindly, not knowing which way to turn. In a sense, I too was paralyzed. I went through my own transformation as little by little I found confidence in myself. It took being thrust out of my comfort zone into a different, unexpected life I knew nothing about to finally find the hidden potential deep inside and become the woman I was capable of becoming.

From the first night of the accident, I didn't know where to go or what to do to help my family, but now I am a stronger, more confident, loving advocate for Reed and Rob, as well as all of my children. I am no longer insecure about my intellectual abilities. I no longer doubt them or compare my knowledge with others'. I know that I am capable of far more than I ever expected. I am a more patient and understanding woman. I am less critical and much more compassionate than ever before. Although I still struggle with depression and fibromyalgia I am better able to control my emotions. When I feel like life is too overwhelming I don't give up or quit; I keep trying. Now I am not afraid to try something new, even difficult. I never thought there was a ghost of a chance I could or would ever write a book!

In what feels like a blink of an eye I have gone from being fearful to hopeful, insecure to confident, poor in spirit to experiencing strong spiritual connections, and I know with assurance that my Lord and Savior will always help me manage whatever life sends my way.

I see the Lord taking the challenges and triumphs of my life and composing a symphony with them. It begins as a simple melody, soft and sweet, adding harmonies as I grow. I gather depth with various musical instruments as each movement of the piece progresses. When the percussion and cymbals crescendo until they make my heart beat with fear, my all-knowing Composer soothes my tears with lovely stringed instruments playing a new melody, no longer simple but sweetly filled with understanding and purpose. My song is not over; there are melodies and movements to include. But since I have learned to trust completely in my Composer I know that any discords will be resolved and my song will continue forever.

Yesterday I was naïve,
My future was still ahead of me,
My dreams were beautiful—rose-colored.
I had goals to work toward,
And life was just what I expected it to be.

Years became decades, and my path was obscured,
My rose-colored dreams turned to painful reality.
It wasn't what I expected life to be.
I lost control of my circumstances,
Or was I ever really in control?
I had to trust in God to lead me
And follow His plan to reach my full potential.

I've come through the darkness into the light of day.
My future is golden.
Heaven's rays shine down on me and show me the way.
My mind, heart, and spirit are at peace
Knowing God will continue to lead me along.

Life—so different than I anticipated,
From the depths of despair to the truest of joys.

The road I have traveled
With its many bends and curves
Has made me a better woman,
Better than I ever expected to be.

Sheryl Nixon, 2009

Raynham Public Library
760 South Main Street
Raynham, MA 02767
raynhampubliclibrary.org
508-823-1344

User name: MacDonald, Eileen Ellen

Title: Lessons : my path to a
meaningful life
Author: Bündchen, Gisele, 1980-
Item ID: 33573001048096
Item Price: $14.56
Date due: 8/4/2021,23:59

itle: In the blink of an eye : the Reed
d Rob Nixon s
hor: Nixon, Sheryl Brown.
ID: 33573000908084
Price: $16.95
Jue: 8/4/2021,23:59

lthy and keep reading!

Epilogue

OUR JOURNEY HAS been an amazing one and we are still experiencing many ups and downs, but through them all we continue to be incredibly blessed. April 4, 2011, marked the sixteenth anniversary of the accident that changed our lives in the blink of an eye. We are still learning as we go along.

Reed keeps busy working on the computer with some on-line businesses he started. His health is relatively stable; we watch his blood sugar closely and he seems to be doing pretty well. Reed is a wonderful guest speaker, sharing his experiences at various engagements. For many years now (since he was just starting out at Bentley) Reed has been a favorite guest lecturer for a legal class on campus, Law and Society.

Together, Reed and his long-time doctor give a seminar each year at the University of Massachusetts for students in the medical field. They teach the up-and-coming medical doctors of the future, explaining ways in which patients with injuries similar to Reed's could and should be treated to improve their quality of life. Reed is also excellent at sharing examples of what *not* to do.

At the conclusion of his lectures or seminars, Reed always leaves time to answer questions. There have been many questions over the years, but the one that stands out in my mind is when a teenage girl asked Reed,

"Did you ever think of committing suicide?"

I'm pretty sure my heart stopped beating at that moment! I was afraid for Reed, wondering if he would answer the question—and if he did, what would he say?

Reed paused for a moment as he pondered the question and how to best answer it. Then he said, "Yes, I thought about it. But I realized I couldn't do anything about it, and I never thought about it again." Reed continues to be a shining example to me of how to turn lemons into lemonade.

Reed also enjoys keeping up with sports. But the thing he loves the most is being an uncle to his sixteen nieces and nephews.

Rob and Katie still live in Irvine, California, where Rob is a senior tax consultant for the accounting firm BDO. He works full-time, and a lot of overtime during tax season. Rob also makes an effort to serve as a guest speaker, sharing the understanding he has gained from his experiences. Katie and Rob try to experience as much in life as they possibly can. In 2010 they vacationed in Thailand with Katie's family. They are very happy together.

2010 Rob and Katie's brother, Stuart in Thailand

This whole ordeal has been such a growing experience for our family. While our challenges and trials have not been easy, we have become better people as a result of them. We have grown emotionally and spiritually to levels that we never knew were possible. And not only have we grown and changed through this incredible journey—innumerable lives have been touched and expanded because of our experiences.

As a result of the accident that was so devastatingly destructive, our whole family is more deeply connected and united, and we have become stronger still. Our level of support has expanded and broadened so that we have a large network of wonderful, loving people we can count on if we ever need them.

2010 family reunion in St. George, Utah

As our children experience the ups and downs of their

lives, they recognize that giving up is never a good option. They've watched Mark and me struggle through and survive the storms of life, and they know that they can, too. Reed and Rob are constant reminders that life is worthwhile and even enjoyable no matter what strange twists and turns it produces.

Mark and I thought we had a good marriage before the accident. But since that devastating night, we have grown to appreciate and admire each other as individuals, recognizing our different strengths and talents. We love each other more deeply and completely than we ever thought possible, and we look forward to spending the rest of our lives together. And whatever surprises come along we plan to enjoy the ride.

I'll Never Stop Loving You

I woke up one morning and looked in the mirror,
Saw gray hairs and wrinkles, and it was real clear
That my youth was over, and middle age, too.
But I've never stopped loving you.

Was it just yesterday we were young and in love,
Waiting for children to come from above?
They came one by one 'til our family was through,
And I couldn't stop loving you.

Yes, they came, they grew up, then they all moved away.
We wondered what we would do day after day.
But we worked hard, then played, and had so much to do,
And I didn't stop loving you.

Let's grow old together, just you and me,
In love forever, eternally.

We'll laugh, live, and learn 'til our journey is through,
And I'll never stop loving you.

We've spent many years rearing children we love,
And now lots of grandkids are sent from above.
We pamper and play 'til our energy's through, and
I still never stop loving you.

I sat after breakfast just watching you read.
Your eyes had grown tired; you wore glasses to see.
You looked up at me, and you gave me a wink,
And again I started to think

Let's grow old together, just you and me,
In love forever, eternally.
We'll laugh, live, and learn 'til our journey is through,
And I'll never stop loving you.

I <u>never will</u> stop loving you.

Sheryl Nixon, 2008

Appendix

Beautiful Baby

Beautiful baby, beautiful child,
Beautiful baby tender and mild
You are the love, the love of my life.
You are the love of a husband and wife.
Beautiful baby, beautiful child,
Beautiful baby tender and mild
I love you so and I want you to know
You will always be my beautiful baby.
Beautiful baby.

Beautiful Baby, Sheryl Nixon, 1997

Midweek Housewife Blues

I woke up this mornin' to the garbage truck roarin' down
the street, I missed him again.
By this time next week that trash will reek and I'll need oxygen.
I've got the floor to mop from that can of pop, spilled the
night before.
My baby who is barely two is smearin' lipstick on the door.

I got the midweek housewife blues.
I got the blues, the midweek housewife blues
From the top of my head down through my shoes.
I got the midweek housewife blues.
The afternoon has come all too soon; my kids are home from school.
Old math is a curse but the new math is worse. I'm feelin' like a fool.
With my achin' head, I'm goin' to bed. I made it through the day.
If I could sleep until next week, I wouldn't have to say
I got the midweek housewife blues.
I got the blues, the midweek housewife blues
From the top of my head down through my shoes
I got the midweek housewife blues.

Midweek Housewife Blues, Sheryl Nixon, 1985

You're His Hero

The other day I watched you and your little boy playing games.
Neither of you noticed I was there.
You both were captivated, and I knew I'd never seen
A father-son relationship to compare.

I love to see him sit like you and comb his hair like yours.
Sometimes he tries to read the paper, too.
He brings you down your slippers. Then he says, "Will you get mine?"
I can tell he's crazy over you.

You're his hero. He watches everything you do.
You're his hero. He wants to be like you.
He'll follow like your shadow
And walk right in your shoes
'Cause you're his hero.

I spend most every day with him from morning until night.
There's no doubt in my mind he loves me too.
But I love to see his face light up when you walk through
the door.
He's runnin' with his arms stretched out to you.

You're his hero. He watches everything you do.
You're his hero. He wants to be like you.
He'll follow like your shadow
And walk right in your shoes
'Cause you're his hero.

You're His Hero, Sheryl Nixon, 1986

Brotherly Love

We made our start a year apart
Just me an' you was all that we knew.
No matter where, we were a pair
Brothers together from the heart.

Though we were small an' not so tall
We spent our time playin' basketball.
We loved to race. We set the pace.
Stayin' together through it all.

'Cause we've got brotherly love, brotherly love.
Ours is a gift sent from heaven above.
Brotherly love, brotherly love
Sent from heaven up above.

One April night, oh what a sight.
We never made it home that night.
We got in a wreck and broke our necks
And learned we were both paralyzed.

Through thick and thin we would wear a grin.
We'd make it through this somehow.
Just do our part with a cheerful heart.
Life would go on anyhow.

Now every day we try to say
Look at your life in a positive way.
We'll make it through, just me an' you
God will help us every day

'Cause we've got brotherly love, brotherly love.
Ours is a gift sent from heaven above.
Brotherly love, brotherly love
Sent from heaven up above.

Brotherly Love, Sheryl Nixon, 1997

Sleepy Head

Sleepyhead, it's time for bed.
I will sing to you until you're fast asleep.
Close your eyes, I won't go away.

Little one, the day is done.
I will hold you gently rocking to and fro
Singing soft this simple melody.
Hush my dear, your mother's near.
Oooo your mother's near.

Sound asleep lost in sweet dreams.
Not a care as long as you know I am there.
Oh how much I love your sleepy head.

Hush my dear, your mother's near.
Oooo your mother's near.

Sleepyhead, Sheryl Nixon, 1984

Look Inward

When life gets you down, as it sometimes will,
And your face wears a frown 'cause you've had your fill
Of the challenges and trials day after day,
And you've 'bout given up, and you don't want to pray.

When you're out of control with no help in sight
And you just wanna quit, but you know it's not right
To desert all of your goals and the life you have led
Just to give up the fight and lie there in bed.

Then it's time to look inward and gather the strength
Of your spirit and soul. Then you'll find at length
In God's precious time, which you do not know,
He knew of your struggles and how much you'd grow.

While workin' hard just to make it through
One day at a time is the best you can do.
But the rest of existence, yes, throughout all time
You'll give praise to God for that chance to climb.

Then living with a life of pain
Will seem but a moment of sorrow and strain.
And the rest of existence, yes, throughout all time
You'll give praise to God for that chance to climb.

Look Inward, Sheryl Nixon, 1996

I Love to Sing

All around the world, doesn't matter where you go,
There's people singin' in the shower or with the radio.
Everyone loves music whether rock or lullaby.
I'm no different from the rest; music gets me high

'Cause more than anything, oh more than anything,
More than anything I love to sing.

It doesn't matter who I'm with or if I'm all alone,
Singin' with my stereo or singin' on my own.
Music makes me happy, makes me feel so good inside.
Hard days don't seem half so bad. I guess that must be why

More than anything, oh more than anything,
More than anything I love to sing.

I sing to make me happy and to cheer me when I'm blue.
And if I feel like givin' up, I sing to help me through.

I try to make life easier and brighten up the day.
As long as I keep singin' I know I'll be okay

'Cause more than anything, oh more than anything,
More than anything I love to sing.

I Love to Sing, Sheryl Nixon, 1986

Together Forever

We're in this together, together forever,
Together 'til the end of time.
Through stormy weather, hangin' in there together,
Somehow it'll turn out fine.
Well, I'll be here to help you through the hard times.
I'll be here in the good times, too.
Hey, we're gonna make it.
Nothin's gonna break it.
Together, baby, me an' you.

We're in this together, together forever.
Darlin', this was meant to be.
There's nothin' I know that will ever make me let go
You've got my guarantee.
Well, no one ever said life was easy
And honey, now we know it's true.
But hey, we're gonna make it.
Nothin's gonna break it.
Together, baby, me an' you.

You an' me, we got a good thing goin'
Through life we'll see that we can keep on growin'

If we stick together like birds of a feather.
Hey, I'll stick with you.

We're in this together, together forever,
Together 'til the end of time.
Through stormy weather, hangin' in there together,
Somehow it'll turn out fine.
Well, I'll be here to help you through the hard times.
I'll be here in the good times, too.
Hey, we're gonna make it.
Nothin's gonna break it.
Together, baby, me an' you.

Hey we're gonna make it.
Nothin's gonna break it.
Together, baby, me an' you.

Together Forever, Sheryl Nixon, 1986

Poem

I remember the day when our lives turned gray,
And the world we knew fell apart.
I sat by your bed, thoughts raced through my head,
A deep, aching throb filled my heart.

You would not be the same as you ever had been.
We would try to accept that now
And pull what strength was inside us
To learn how to cope somehow.

As weeks go by, it's hard not to cry,

But we work to get through each day.
When we feel all alone in our twilight zone,
We remember the need to pray.

We open our hearts to the Lord, Jesus Christ
And pray for strength through Him.
Then work like it all depends on us
But pray like it depends on Him.

Sheryl Nixon, 1995

Angel of Light

Every now and then, or maybe once in a lifetime,
We might find someone unique, unlike the rest,
Who's Christ-like, one who loves and one who cares,
One who offers help we need.

Every now and then or maybe once in a lifetime,
We might find someone who's willing to give,
Unselfishly, all they have, all they know,
All to make sure we succeed.

Angel of Light, that's what you are.
You've given me so much love.
Throughout my life you'll seem to be
An Angel of Light from above.

If every now and then or maybe once in a lifetime
I could be to someone like you have been to me
Christ-like, willing to share, willing to give,
Wanting to feel, wanting to live, and serve like you served me.

Angel of Light, that's what you are.
You've given me so much love.
Throughout my life you'll seem to be
An Angel of Light from above.

Now through my life I'll try to be
An Angel of Light from above.

Angel of Light, Sheryl Nixon, 1989

Never Give Up

Never give up the fight for right. Never give up at all.
Never give up the will to win, to stand up when you fall.
Never give up your heritage, you came from royal birth.
And always remember why you came to Earth.

Before we came to Earth to live we started with a plan.
Our Father up in heaven took us each one by the hand.
He promised us eternal life if we would choose His way
And then He said, "Remember, I'll be here when you pray."

Now we've all forgotten the life we used to share.
We don't remember promises of Father way back there.
To some it seems like this Earth life is all there'll ever be.
But Father's up there waiting, patiently, to see who will

Never give up the fight for right. Never give up at all.
Never give up the will to win, to stand up when you fall.
Never give up your heritage, you came from royal birth.
And always remember why you came to Earth.

We are here to prove ourselves. Will we live righteously?
The choices we make in our lives decide our destiny.
Endure throughout the good and bad, that's what we're asked to do.
And if we prove we're faithful, we'll be among those who will

Never give up the fight for right. Never give up at all.
Never give up the will to win, to stand up when you fall.
Never give up your heritage, you came from royal birth.
And always remember why you came to Earth.

Never Give Up, Sheryl Nixon, 1986

One Day at a Time

When I was just a little girl, I fell and hurt my knee.
And I was just about as sad as a little girl could be.
I had to use a wheelchair, then crutches every day,
And when I'd get discouraged, I'd hear my mama say,

You just take it one day at a time.
One day, just one day at a time.
'Cause anything is possible, yeah, anything could be
By takin' one simply one day at a time.

Then before I knew it I was nearly thirty-three.
Tryin' to raise a family, I had little time for me.
With many trips to doctors, and school every day,
I'd find myself discouraged, and I'd hear my mama say,

You just take it one day at a time.

<![CDATA[◄ SHERYL BROWN NIXON]]>

One day, just one day at a time.
'Cause anything is possible, yeah anything could be
By takin' one simply one day at a time.

You can eat an elephant if you take one bite at a time.
You can earn a living if you save up every dime.
You can cross a mountain top if every step you climb.
Don't give up! Soon you're gonna find

You just take it one day at a time.
One day, just one day at a time.
'Cause anything is possible, yeah anything could be
By takin' one simply one day at a time.

'Cause anything is possible, yeah anything could be
By takin' one, only one, one merely one,
Takin' one simply one day at a time.

One Day at a Time, Sheryl Nixon, 1998

What Will I Give This Christmastime

What will I give this Christmastime when so much has been given to me?
What will I sacrifice of mine so that others may receive?
My life has not been without trials, and sorrow I have seen.
And yet I've been so blessed because of love that's been given to me.
So what will I give this Christmastime, presents or money or toys?
What should I give to friends of mine to bring them the greatest joy?

Peace of heart. Peace of mind. Peace from worldly care.
Peace to make it through life's trials, peace is what I'd
share.

But how do I give this gift of peace that we try so hard to
find?
It comes through the light of Jesus Christ, the Son of God
divine.
As I live through pain and heartache, with faith and trust
in the Lord,
I find the peace He promises, the peace that He sends
with His word.

So I'll share the light of Jesus Christ humbly and never
cease.
What will I give this Christmastime? I'll give this gift of
peace.

What Will I Give This Christmastime, Sheryl Nixon, 1998

Why Me

Every mornin' I wake up and stumble out of bed
Lookin' for some aspirin to soothe my achin' head.
The night before I wondered how I'd face another day.
But here I am this mornin' just tryin' to find my way.

I never did consider what I'd ever do
If my life turned upside down, how would I get through?
Could faith and hope help me survive? 'Cause I could not
turn back.
Or would I get discouraged and maybe start to ask

Why me? Why me? Would I then begin to ask
Why me? Why me? Life is so unfair.

When I look at others and their adversity
Many live with sorrow, and some have known defeat.
And so I have to tell myself, "I am not alone,
'Cause people all around the world have troubles of their
own."

Why me? Why me? Every day they ask themselves
Why me? Why me? Life is so unfair.

My own heartaches still remain, but I try to understand
Trials can bring out my best if I give the Lord my hand
And let Him guide me every day 'til I finally see
Blessings have resulted from the trials given me.

Every mornin' I wake up and my knees hit the floor.
I offer my most humble prayer and thank the Lord before
I hurry on throughout my day, and I try to see
The many gifts of love and peace He has given me.

Why me? Why me? Why have I been blessed so much?
Why me? Why me? I have more than my share.

Why Me, Sheryl Nixon, 2006

More Than I Deserve

I love your tender care. I love it when you brush my hair.
And all the time you share with me.
And when I'm feeling blue, I know that I can lean on you.

And sometimes, you cry, too, with me.

You're all that I want, everything that I need
And more, much more than I deserve.
Every day when I awake, I know there's no mistake
You're more, much more than I deserve.

I love you. Oh how I love you. You love me, too.

Sometimes I'm tired at night and you come to me and
hold me tight.
You make the day end right for me.
A marriage filled with love. We seem to fit like hand in glove.
I thank the Lord above for you.

You're all that I want, everything that I need
And more, much more than I deserve.
Every day when I awake, I know there's no mistake
You're more, much more than I deserve.

I love you. Oh, how I love you. You love me, too.

More Than I Deserve, Sheryl Nixon, 1984

Do Ye Even as I

I watched Him from a distance, the one they called the
teacher.
And as I drew near Him I heard, "Do ye even as I."
I saw the little children linger by His side.
With a gentle, loving smile
He said, "Do ye even as I."

I saw Him forgive the sinner. With great compassion He led.
To the sad heart, He was comforter. Unto us all He said,
"Do ye even as I. For then ye shall receive
All the blessings Father hath for those who follow me."

I saw Him feed five thousand with two fish and some bread.
He showed love to the homeless. "Do ye even as I," He said.
He suffered in the garden so we'd have eternal life.
Jesus drank the bitter cup and said, "Do ye even as I."

I saw Him forgive the sinner. With great compassion He led.
To the sad heart, He was comforter. Unto us all He said,
"Do ye even as I. For then ye shall receive
All the blessings Father hath for those who follow me."

He sacrificed more than we comprehend.
He asked only our heart in return.
He gave up His life, as was prophesied.
He was the chosen one.

He showed me what I could be.

I saw Him forgive the sinner. With great compassion He led.
To the sad heart, He was comforter. Unto us all He said,
"Do ye even as I. For then ye shall receive
All the blessings Father hath for those who follow me.

All the blessings Father hath for those who follow me."

Do Ye Even as I, Sheryl Nixon, 1990

Fightin' Dragons All Day

I wake up late, gotta get the kids to school,
Racin' to work, breakin' every traffic rule.
I don't have time to do the things I should.
I never expected this was motherhood.

'Cause I work all day, don't have time for play,
And I know I'm getting' older 'cause my hair is turnin'
gray
From fightin' dragons all day.
I'm fightin' dragons all day.

Sheryl Nixon, 1986

I Know God Lives

I remember scriptures that my mother read to me
Like Moses and the Israelites and how God set them free.
She also told me of a man whose life was free from sin.
Then she shared the testimony she had gained of Him.

I know God lives. I know His plan.
I know through Jesus Christ, Father's work began.
I know He lived and died for me,
So I could be with Him eternally.

Through the coming years, I get to teach about His word.
I'll try to share His love, and I will do my best to serve.
I'll search for those who seek for Jesus Christ, to find His
way,
Teach His gospel truths, and be a witness for His name.

My faith in God has strengthened; I've found power in
His word,
And now the time has come for me to go and serve the
Lord.
All my life I've waited, waited for this day,
Waited for the time when I could stand alone and say,

"I know God lives! I know His plan!
I know through Jesus Christ, Father's work began!
I know He lived and died for me,
So I could be with Him eternally."

I know He lives, and He loves me.
I want to be with Him eternally.

I Know God Lives, Sheryl Nixon, 1999

Serving the Best I Can

Each day I see so many souls searching for the truth.
Some are in the prime of life, some still in their youth.
I want so much to share with them the joy I feel inside
Knowing I've a Savior who will always be my guide

When my neighbor passes me I smile as he goes by.
I hope he'll see that I love life and maybe wonder why.
So if I have the answers and know what I should do
I'll be a good example of the things I know are true.

And be an instrument in Thy hand, serving my fellowman,
Spreading the gospel plan my whole life through.
A humble instrument in Thy hand, serving the best I can

Help others understand the gospel's true.

When I help someone in need, I'll do it with a smile,
Give the best I've got to give, and go the second mile.
Through service love and friendship, I've found that there's
a key.
By my serving others, I am really serving Thee.

I'll be an instrument in Thy hand, serving my fellowman,
Spreading the gospel plan my whole life through.
A humble instrument in Thy hand, serving the best I can
Help others understand the gospel's true.
The gospel's true.

Serving the Best I Can, Sheryl Nixon, 1989

Focus on the Blessings

Looking back the past twelve months, my life has really
changed.
Everything that once seemed good has all been rearranged.
Every day I've prayed for strength and watched for peace
ahead,
But bad gets worse and I cry out, "I wish that I was dead!"

"Oh how much longer can I go on?" I ask the Lord, "How
long?"
And all I hear inside my head is, "Patience child, hold on.
I know that you can't see me now, and yet I'm always
here.
Although you may not understand, I have a plan, my dear.

You must think about the good things and trust I know
what's best.
Just think about the good things, and I will do the rest."
The answer came so clearly, right there inside my head,
And I knew exactly what to do when I was tormented.

I must focus on the blessings the Lord has given me.
Focus on the blessings, for that is when I see
That when my mind is full of doubt and I just want to
scream and shout,
If I focus on the blessings, the Lord will give me peace.

Now when I'm overburdened and life seems so unfair
And I begin to wonder if Father is really there,
I gather up my burden and lay it at His throne
And pray with deep thanksgiving for everything He's done.

Then I focus on the blessings the Lord has given me.
Focus on the blessings, for that is when I see
That when my mind is full of doubt and I just want to
scream and shout,
If I focus on the blessings, the Lord will give me peace.
When I focus on the blessings, the Lord will give me peace.

Focus On the Blessings, words by Sheryl Nixon, 2003,
music by Kent Nixon, 2010

You Shall Have Peace in Me

Can you tell me where to turn for peace? Somehow I've
lost my way.
And it's so hard to understand the pain I have to face each day.

I try to gather strength and courage to help me carry on,
But it seems insufficient when day is finally done.

Can you tell me where to turn for peace? Sometimes I feel
alone.
And though I give all that I have to give, I can't make it
on my own.
I want to feel the Holy Spirit to help me make it through.
I've read and pondered scriptures; Lord, tell me what to do.

"Walk in the meekness of My spirit, and you shall have
peace in Me.
When the night is dark and full of sorrow, I'll hold you tenderly.
I'll bear you up as on eagles' wings if you wait patiently.
Fear not little child, you shall have peace in Me."

Could it be He could lighten my load?
How I yearn to know such peace.
So I pray with faith that through Him
My own strength will increase.

Now I know where I can turn for peace. I think I understand.
Difficulties will not hold me back when I'm holding Thy
hand.
Though I may not be freed from challenge and still must
give my all,
As long as Thou art with me, I know I will stand tall

And walk in the meekness of Thy spirit and I shall have
peace in Thee.
When the night is dark and full of sorrow, Thou wilt comfort me

And bear me up as on eagles' wings. I will wait patiently.
I love Thee dear Lord. I have found peace in Thee.

You Shall Have Peace in Me, Sheryl Nixon, 2003

An Eternal Family to Love

Today my heart is filled with joy as I sit in the Lord's sacred house
And look at each of my children, along with my eternal spouse.

The gospel plan brings families together forever, that's the principle I have learned,
But it certainly hasn't come easily, and for each of us it has to be earned.

Today my heart is filled with a peace that can only come from the Lord
For trying to keep His commandments and living each day by His word.

Now I certainly am not perfect, and I've worked through trials and strife,
But once in a while there comes a time when contentment encompasses my life.

Today is that day, and I feel a deep love for God and His son Jesus Christ
For sending me an eternal family to love and cherish all my life.

Sheryl Nixon, 2007

The Race

I tighten my shoes, strap my number on,
I hear the gun go off, then everybody's gone
For the finish line.
This race is mine.

I start way too fast. I gotta pull it back,
Wait for my time 'til I'm ready to attack,
Feel the runner's high
As I pass 'em by.

The thought in my mind says I'll never be left behind.

I'm gonna win the race. No, second place won't be good
enough.
I know I'm tougher than who I was before.
And I will seize the day, put my trophy upon display,
So I can show everyone who's number one.

I wake up, my old life's gone.
Disappointment and anger I ponder, but they won't do to
get me through.
I start therapy. It makes me a little stronger.
Some of life's trials will be life long, but I still have life, so
I'll live it right.

The trophy by my door says I've never given up before.

I'm gonna win the race. No, second place won't be good
enough.
I know I'm tougher than who I was before.

And I will seize the day, put my trophy upon display,
So I can show everyone who's number one.

I know what it's like to be an "underdog."
My daddy taught me to put my faith in God.
So every goal I set with no regret will help me to the time
When I cross the line.

I'm gonna win the race. No, second place won't be good
enough.
I know I'm tougher than who I was before.
And I will seize the day, put my trophy upon display,
So I can show everyone who's number one.

The Race, Kent Mark Nixon, 2009

Poem

Yesterday I was naïve,
My future was still ahead of me,
My dreams were beautiful—rose-colored.
I had goals to work toward,
And life was just what I expected it to be.
Years became decades, and my path was obscured,
My rose-colored dreams turned to painful reality.
It wasn't what I expected life to be.

I lost control of my circumstances,
Or was I ever really in control?
I had to trust in God to lead me
And follow His plan to reach my full potential.

I've come through the darkness into the light of day.
My future is golden.
Heaven's rays shine down on me and show me the way.
My mind, heart, and spirit are at peace
Knowing God will continue to lead me along.

Life—so different than I anticipated,
From the depths of despair to the truest of joys.

The road I have traveled
With its many bends and curves
Has made me a better woman,
Better than I ever expected to be.

Sheryl Nixon, 2009

I'll Never Stop Loving You

I woke up one morning and looked in the mirror,
Saw gray hairs and wrinkles, and it was real clear
That my youth was over, and middle-age, too.
But I've never stopped loving you.

Was it just yesterday we were young and in love,
Waiting for children to come from above?
They came one by one 'til our family was through,
And I couldn't stop loving you.

Yes, they came, they grew up, then they all moved away.
We wondered what we would do day after day.
But we worked hard, then played, and had so much to do,
And I didn't stop loving you.

Let's grow old together, just you and me,
In love forever, eternally.
We'll laugh, live, and learn 'til our journey is through,
And I'll never stop loving you.

We've spent many years rearing children we love,
And now lots of grandkids are sent from above.
We pamper and play 'til our energy's through, and
I still never stop loving you.

I sat after breakfast just watching you read.
Your eyes had grown tired; you wore glasses to see.
You looked up at me, and you gave me a wink,
And again I started to think

Let's grow old together, just you and me,
In love forever, eternally.
We'll laugh, live, and learn 'til our journey is through,
And I'll never stop loving you.

I <u>never will</u> stop loving you.

Sheryl Nixon, 2008

For more information or
for questions and comments
for any of the Nixons
please visit us on the web at
sherylnixon.com.

CPSIA information can be obtained at www.ICGtesting.com
Printed in the USA
LVOW08s0922180813

348440LV00003B/278/P